100 Great Activities: The best of the Cambridge Handbooks for Language Teachers

Cambridge Handbooks for Language Teachers

This series, now with over 50 titles, offers practical ideas, techniques and activities for the teaching of English and other languages, providing inspiration for both teachers and trainers.

Recent titles in this series:

Teach Business English
SYLVIE DONNA

Teaching English Spelling
A practical guide
RUTH SHEMESH and SHEILA WALLER

Using Folktales
ERIC K. TAYLOR

Learner English (Second edition)
A teacher's guide to interference and other problems
EDITED BY MICHAEL SWAN and BERNARD SMITH

Planning Lessons and Courses
Designing sequences of work for the language classroom
TESSA WOODWARD

Teaching Large Multilevel Classes
NATALIE HESS

Using the Board in the Language Classroom
JEANNINE DOBBS

Writing Simple Poems
Pattern poetry for language acquisition
VICKI L. HOLMES and MARGARET R. MOULTON

Laughing Matters
Humour in the language classroom
PÉTER MEDGYES

Stories
Narrative activities in the language classroom
RUTH WAJNRYB

Using Authentic Video in the Language Classroom
JANE SHERMAN

Extensive Reading Activities for Teaching Language
EDITED BY JULIAN BAMFORD and RICHARD R. DAY

Language Activities for Teenagers
EDITED BY SETH LINDSTROMBERG

Pronunciation Practice Activities
A resource book for teaching English pronunciation
MARTIN HEWINGS

Drama Techniques (Third edition)
A resource book of communication activities for language teachers
ALAN MALEY and ALAN DUFF

Five-Minute Activities for Business English
PAUL EMMERSON and NICK HAMILTON

Games for Language Learning (Third edition)
ANDREW WRIGHT, DAVID BETTERIDGE and MICHAEL BUCKBY

Dictionary Activities
CINDY LEANEY

Dialogue Activities
Exploring spoken interaction in the language class
NICK BILBROUGH

Five-Minute Activities for Young Learners
PENNY MCKAY and JENNI GUSE

The Internet and the Language Classroom (Second edition)
A practical guide for teachers
GAVIN DUDENEY

Working with Images
A resource book for the language classroom
BEN GOLDSTEIN

Grammar Practice Activities (Second edition)
A practical guide for teachers
PENNY UR

Intercultural Language Activities
JOHN CORBETT

Learning One-to-One
INGRID WISNIEWSKA

Communicative Activities for EAP
JENNI GUSE

Memory Activities for Language Learning
NICK BILBROUGH

Vocabulary Activities
PENNY UR

Classroom Management Techniques
JIM SCRIVENER

CLIL Activities
A resource for subject and language teachers
LIZ DALE and ROSIE TANNER

Language Learning with Technology
Ideas for integrating technology in the classroom
GRAHAM STANLEY

Translation and Own-language Activities
PHILIP KERR

Language Learning with Digital Video
BEN GOLDSTEIN and PAUL DRIVER

Discussions and More
Oral fluency practice in the classroom
PENNY UR

Interaction Online
Creative activities for blended learning
LINDSAY CLANDFIELD and JILL HADFIELD

Activities for Very Young Learners
HERBERT PUCHTA and KAREN ELLIOTT

Teaching and Developing Reading Skills
PETER WATKINS

Lexical Grammar
Activities for teaching chunks and exploring patterns
LEO SELIVAN

Off the Page
Activities to bring lessons alive and enhance learning
CRAIG THAINE

Teaching in Challenging Circumstances
CHRIS SOWTON

Teaching and Developing Writing Skills
CRAIG THAINE

100 Great Activities: The best of the Cambridge Handbooks for Language Teachers

Edited by Penny Ur and Scott Thornbury

Shaftesbury Road, Cambridge CB2 8EA, United Kingdom

One Liberty Plaza, 20th Floor, New York, NY 10006, USA

477 Williamstown Road, Port Melbourne, VIC 3207, Australia

314–321, 3rd Floor, Plot 3, Splendor Forum, Jasola District Centre, New Delhi – 110025, India

103 Penang Road, #05–06/07, Visioncrest Commercial, Singapore 238467

Cambridge University Press & Assessment is a department of the University of Cambridge.

We share the University's mission to contribute to society through the pursuit of education, learning and research at the highest international levels of excellence.

www.cambridge.org
Information on this title: www.cambridge.org/9781009348737

© Cambridge University Press & Assessment 2024

This publication is in copyright. Subject to statutory exception and to the provisions of relevant collective licensing agreements, no reproduction of any part may take place without the written permission of Cambridge University Press & Assessment.

First published 2024

20 19 18 17 16 15 14 13 12 11 10 9 8 7 6 5 4 3 2 1

Printed in Great Britain by CPI Group (UK) Ltd, Croydon CR0 4YY

A catalogue record for this publication is available from the British Library

ISBN 978-1-009-34873-7 Paperback
ISBN 978-1-009-34874-4 eBook
ISBN 978-1-009-34875-1 Cambridge Core

Cambridge University Press & Assessment has no responsibility for the persistence or accuracy of URLs for external or third-party internet websites referred to in this publication and does not guarantee that any content on such websites is, or will remain, accurate or appropriate.

Contents

Thanks		viii
Acknowledgements		ix
Foreword		xi
Introduction		I

1 Speaking — 5

1.1	30-second stimulus talks	*Language Activities for Teenagers*	6
1.2	Alibi	*Lessons from Nothing*	8
1.3	All-purpose needs check	*Teach Business English*	10
1.4	Becoming a picture	*Drama Techniques 3rd edition*	12
1.5	Chants	*Discussions and More*	14
1.6	Congratulations	*Personalizing Language Learning*	16
1.7	Course evaluation	*Ways of Doing*	17
1.8	Describe and draw	*Pictures for Language Learning*	18
1.9	Dialogue interpretation	*Drama Techniques 3rd edition*	19
1.10	Discussion group tag	*Off the Page*	21
1.11	Find someone who	*Keep Talking*	22
1.12	Flashing	*Five-Minute Activities*	24
1.13	Getting students to ask the questions	*Classroom Management Techniques*	25
1.14	Guess the animal in 20 questions	*Five-Minute Activities for Young Learners*	26
1.15	How do they rank?	*Teaching Adult Second Language Learners*	27
1.16	Interview interrogatives	*Teach Business English*	28
1.17	Make them say it	*The Standby Book*	30
1.18	Management tips	*Five-Minute Activities for Business English*	32
1.19	Map-reading: the treasure hunt	*Testing Spoken Language*	33
1.20	Multipart story drama	*Using Folktales*	35
1.21	Name them	*Discussions and More*	36
1.22	Numbers in my life	*Personalizing Language Learning*	38
1.23	Opinion poll	*Keep Talking*	40
1.24	PMI	*Keep Talking*	42
1.25	Pronouncing places, products and planets	*Pronunciation Practice Activities*	43
1.26	Recorded stories	*Language Learning with Technology*	45
1.27	Say things about a picture	*Discussions and More*	46

100 Great Activities: The Best of the Cambridge Handbooks for Language Teachers

1.28	Secret topic	*Keep Talking*	49
1.29	Self-directed interviews	*Keep Talking*	50
1.30	Speed dating	*Dialogue Activities*	51
1.31	Spoken journals	*Language Learning with Technology*	53
1.32	Tell me my story	*Learning One-to-One*	55
1.33	Three things about me	*Teaching Large Multilevel Classes*	56
1.34	What are the differences?	*Keep Talking*	57
1.35	What do we have in common?	*Learning One-to-One*	59
1.36	Why do you have a monkey in your bag?	*Five-Minute Activities*	61

2 Listening — 63

2.1	Altering and marking	*Teaching Listening Comprehension*	64
2.2	Change chairs	*Lessons from Nothing*	66
2.3	Ground-plans	*Teaching Listening Comprehension*	67
2.4	Interrupting the story	*Five-Minute Activities*	69
2.5	It happened to me	*Once upon a Time*	70
2.6	Jumbled statements	*Using Authentic Video in the Language Classroom*	71
2.7	Obeying instructions	*Teaching Listening Comprehension*	72
2.8	Oral retelling by students	*Using Folktales*	73
2.9	Predictive listening	*Using Newspapers in the Classroom*	74
2.10	Talk like a robot	*Activities for Very Young Learners*	76
2.11	The teacher's autobiography	*Dictation*	77
2.12	True or false	*Pictures for Language Learning*	78

3 Reading — 79

3.1	An A–Z of signs in English	*Intercultural Language Activities*	80
3.2	Celebrity dinner party	*The Internet and the Language Classroom*	82
3.3	Classroom language	*Working with Words*	84
3.4	Strip cloze	*Using Newspapers in the Classroom*	86
3.5	Using symbols	*Teaching and Developing Reading Skills*	88
3.6	Vanishing stories	*Once upon a Time*	90

4 Writing — 93

4.1	Acrostic	*Writing Simple Poems*	94
4.2	Bingo	*Teaching English Spelling*	96
4.3	Bouncing dialogue	*Games for Language Learning 3rd edition*	97
4.4	Cinquain	*Writing Simple Poems*	99
4.5	Collective story writing	*Teaching in Challenging Circumstances*	101
4.6	Comment on the comments	*Language Learning with Digital Video*	102
4.7	Creative copying	*Beginning to Write*	103
4.8	Delayed reverse translations	*Translation and Own-language Activities*	105
4.9	Dictogloss	*Dictation*	107
4.10	Foodies	*Interaction Online*	108

vi

Contents

4.11	I am ...	*Working with Images*	110
4.12	I can't spell that!	*Memory Activities for Language Learning*	112
4.13	Letters	*Literature in the Language Classroom*	113
4.14	Making mine long	*Teaching Large Multilevel Classes*	114
4.15	Mini-stories	*Dictionary Activities*	115
4.16	Once upon a time	*Extensive Reading Activities for Teaching Language*	116
4.17	Paper talk	*Dialogue Activities*	117
4.18	Point of view	*Stories*	119
4.19	Running dictation	*Communicative Activities for EAP*	121
4.20	Sad consequences	*Laughing Matters*	122
4.21	Simple selfies	*Teaching and Developing Writing Skills*	123
4.22	Summarising the summary	*Literature in the Language Classroom*	125
4.23	Thoughts	*Using Newspapers in the Classroom*	126

5   Vocabulary   **127**

5.1	A long and growing list	*Games for Language Learning 3rd edition*	128
5.2	Association webs	*Using the Board in the Language Classroom*	130
5.3	Connect two	*Vocabulary Activities*	132
5.4	Desirable qualities	*Personalizing Language Learning*	133
5.5	Do you remember?	*Using the Board in the Language Classroom*	135
5.6	Guess them fast!	*Vocabulary Activities*	136
5.7	How many things can you think of that ... ?	*Five-Minute Activities*	138
5.8	Input enhancement	*Lexical Grammar*	139
5.9	Looking up words you know	*Planning Lessons and Courses*	141
5.10	Odd one out	*CLIL Activities*	142
5.11	Pass it round	*Vocabulary Activities*	144
5.12	Search a page	*Vocabulary Activities*	146

6   Grammar   **147**

6.1	Adjectives on the internet	*Grammar Practice Activities*	148
6.2	Circle comparisons	*Grammar Practice Activities*	149
6.3	Drawing my natural world	*Five-Minute Activities for Young Learners*	150
6.4	I see ... You see	*The Standby Book*	151
6.5	Let's have a drink	*Dialogue Activities*	152
6.6	Miming adverbs	*Five-Minute Activities*	153
6.7	Oh!	*Grammar Practice Activities*	154
6.8	Question stories	*Games for Language Learning 3rd edition*	156
6.9	Sentence repetition	*Testing Spoken Language*	158
6.10	Student-generated test	*Learner Autonomy*	159
6.11	What can you do with it?	*Games for Language Learning 3rd edition*	160

Cambridge Handbooks for Language Teachers: Complete Series List   **161**

Index   **164**

vii

Thanks

The editors wish to thank all the authors who have contributed to the *Handbooks* series over the years, and to this collection in particular: their contribution to the quality and long life of the series is inestimable. We also owe a huge debt to the series' founders, Adrian du Plessis and Michael Swan, for blazing the trail we subsequently followed: this book is testimony to their pioneering vision.

We would also like to thank the publishing team at Cambridge: Karen Momber and Jo Timerick, for overseeing the project and sustaining our commitment to it throughout the often complex processes it entailed, and Greg Sibley, for his dedicated attention to detail during the editing process.

Acknowledgements

The authors and publishers acknowledge the following sources of copyright material and are grateful for the permissions granted. While every effort has been made, it has not always been possible to identify the sources of all the material used, or to trace all copyright holders. If any omissions are brought to our notice, we will be happy to include the appropriate acknowledgements on reprinting and in the next update to the digital edition, as applicable.

Key: L = Left, R = Right, T = Top, B = Below.

Text

David Godwin Associates for the poem 'A Martian Sends a Postcard Home' on p.111 from *A Martian Sends A Postcard Home* by Craig Raine. Copyright © Craig Raine, 1979. Reproduced by permission of David Godwin Associates.

Photography

All the photographs are sourced from Getty Images.

p. 34: FrankRamspott/DigitalVision Vectors; p. 81 (TL): Gunter Lenz/imageBROKER; p. 81 (BL): John Seaton Callahan/Moment; p. 81 (TR): Simon McGill/Moment; p. 81 (BR): Owen Franken/ Photodisc; p. 124 (TL): Una Berzina/EyeEm; p. 124 (BL): Oscar Wong/Moment; p. 124 (TR): SDI Productions/E+; p. 124 (BR): Henrik Sorensen/DigitalVision.

Illustrations

Illustrations by QBS Learning.

Typeset

Typesetting by QBS Learning.

Foreword

By Michael Swan

The *Handbooks* series first saw the light of day at a high-level meeting in the late 1970s. To be precise, at 8,230 feet above sea level. My friend Adrian du Plessis and I were on a walking trip in the French Alps. Adrian had been recently appointed by CUP to establish an ELT list; I was one of his new authors. Towards the end of the trip we were overtaken by storms, and had to spend two days in a mountain hut until the weather eased. In the intervals between eating and sleeping, we did a good deal of talking. After exhausting the obvious topics – early lives, education, girlfriends, health, wives, children, travel, favourite writers, etc. etc. – we were driven back to talking about work, a subject which we had been avoiding throughout the trip. We began discussing possible future titles for Adrian's list, and this led on to the notion of a comprehensive range of books covering all the main areas of interest to language teachers. And so the series was born.

The wind finally dropped, and we headed back downhill to the world of work. Memories of the mountains faded into the background, but the series idea remained very present, and Adrian and I had several lower-level meetings to firm up our ideas. We saw the potential series as occupying a middle ground for language teachers. There were plenty of books around introducing teachers to applied linguistics, and any number of recipe books with ideas for one or other kind of classroom activity. But at the time there was comparatively little to bridge the gap between the academic and the purely practical. We envisaged a set of books written by and for practitioners, which would introduce valuable activities framed in general principles that teachers could build on, without going so far up the theoretical scale as to lose touch with the classroom.

It was a very ambitious project. We drew up a list of the main topics we felt we should cover – grammar, vocabulary, pronunciation, the traditional 'four skills', and their subdivisions – and started exploring ways of tracking down suitable authors. Like all ambitious projects, it didn't work out quite as we had expected, and we found ourselves becoming reactive rather than proactive. If we failed to find an author for one topic, someone magically turned up for another, through a recommendation or by pure chance. And as the reputation of the Cambridge ELT list grew under Adrian's management, potential authors began to submit proposals, and we were able to add more and more books. I was privileged in being able to work with some very gifted and experienced practitioners, and I invariably learnt more from our association than they did – as of course editors should. Indeed, the very first book I edited, Penny Ur's remarkable *Discussions that Work*, has influenced my own professional thinking to this day.

Looking at the series today, and the range of topics represented in this collection, I am awestruck by the remarkable success that it has achieved, bringing so much of value into the work of so many teachers. Under the wise and skilful guidance of the editors who followed me, the *Handbooks* series has retained the principles behind the original concept, and brought to fruition the ambitions that germinated in that mountain hut all those years ago. I am proud to have been involved in its beginning.

Introduction

This book is a collection of some of the best activities that have appeared in the nearly 45 years' lifespan of the *Cambridge Handbooks for Language Teachers* series. In order to tap into the phenomenally rich source of teaching practice that the series represents, we have assembled a selection of the most popular activities into a single volume. In this way, teachers who are already familiar with the ideas will have them at their fingertips, while newer teachers will be equipped with a handy 'starting pack' of tried-and-tested activities with which to extend and enrich their current practice. Accordingly, each of the series' authors was invited to submit their personal favourites from their own books, and to provide short comments to explain their choices. From this long list, the editors selected the 100 activities that ultimately make up the book, basing their choices on criteria that are outlined below, while trying to ensure minimal overlap and an ample coverage of teaching objectives. The resulting selection reflects not only the range and quality of the series itself, but, we believe, also represents the essence of good language teaching practice over nearly half a century.

The Cambridge Handbooks for Language Teachers: A brief history

Adrian du Plessis, the first head of ELT publishing at Cambridge University Press, records that the seed of the idea of producing a series of methodology texts for teachers was planted after a fact-finding mission to West Africa in the early 1970s, and further developed in collaboration with Michael Swan (see the *Foreword*). The intention was to fill a gap in the market that no other publishers seemed at the time to be addressing in any consistent fashion. Accordingly, the Cambridge ELT publishing list for 1979 'included the first titles in what was to become an important part of the Press list: practical books for teachers' (Du Plessis 2013 p. 54). The first of these, Alan Maley and Alan Duff's successful *Drama Techniques in Language Learning* (1978), established the basic model: 'a short theoretical introduction with the rest of the book consisting of practical ideas for use in the classroom' (ibid.). Andrew Wright, David Betteridge and Michael Buckby adopted this formula for their equally popular *Games for Language Learning* (1979). Seeing the potential that this model offered, Du Plessis enlisted Michael Swan to become the first editor of a new series, to be called *Cambridge Handbooks for Language Teachers* (CHLT). The series was officially launched in 1981, and was to become 'a crucial part of the Cambridge list and a major contribution to the profession' (Du Plessis, ibid.).

Under Michael Swan's stewardship, the list grew steadily, and included what were to become 'classic' *Handbooks* titles, written by some of the most innovative voices in ELT during the formative years of the communicative approach. Such iconic communicative activities as 'Find someone who' (in Friedericke Klippel's *Keep Talking*, first published in 1984) and 'Describe and draw' (in Andrew Wright's *Pictures for Language Learning,* 1989), along with imaginative ways of rehabilitating dictations (in Paul Davis and Mario Rinvolucri's *Dictation*, 1988), inspired a new generation of language teachers. Michael Swan's tenure also saw the publication of the indispensable collection of contrastive analyses of English and other languages, called *Learner English* (1987), co-edited by

100 Great Activities: The Best of the Cambridge Handbooks for Language Teachers

Swan and Bernard Smith (but not represented in this current volume, since – unlike other titles in the series – it is not a book of activities). Many of the titles in this first wave of *Handbooks* have since been re-published in second or even third editions.

Penny Ur took over the editorship in 1995 and, over the course of the next ten years, added over 20 more titles to the series, covering a wide range of media (such as newspapers, folktales, poems and the internet), and of teaching contexts, including business, ESOL, teenagers and large multilevel classes. Increasingly, *Handbooks* titles were appearing on recommended reading lists for pre- and in-service training courses, as well as occupying the shelves in many teachers' rooms worldwide. Their popularity was further enhanced by the prominent role played by many of the writers at national and international conferences: Mario Rinvolucri, Alan Maley, Andrew Wright, Tessa Woodward and Péter Medgyes, among others.

Penny Ur relinquished the editorship to Scott Thornbury in 2005, and since that time the series has been extended to include around 50 titles in all, many reflecting recent innovations in educational technology and in methodology, including CLIL, online interaction, intercultural competence and own-language use. At the same time, new titles addressing some of the 'core' aspects of language teaching, such as the teaching of reading and writing skills (by Peter Watkins and Craig Thaine, respectively) and classroom management (by Jim Scrivener) have proved very popular. And 2016 saw the launch of the *Pocket Books*, a 'series within the series'; there are now over a dozen titles in this series (although they are not represented in this current selection since they are not activities-based).

The *Handbooks* series continues to thrive while remaining true to its foundational principle of providing practising teachers with well-grounded, practical ideas for immediate classroom application. For a full list of titles in the *Handbooks* series see pages 161–163.

What makes a good language teaching activity?

The language teaching activities in this book were chosen according to a number of criteria, which are listed below, with some explanatory comments. It should be noted that these criteria were seen as guidelines for selection rather than strict rules, and it was not expected that every activity would tick all the boxes.

1 **Plausibility/face validity:** Does the activity seem plausible to teachers? Does it match teachers' professional judgement as to what works in the classroom? Likewise, from the learners' point of view, does the activity seem like something worth doing? The extent to which it satisfies these requirements will impact on the teacher's capacity to 'sell' the activity to the learners, and the learners' willingness to engage with it.

2 **Likely learning value:** How rich is the activity in terms of the amount of language practice it provides? If it involves speaking or writing, how much language does the activity generate? If it involves listening or reading, how much meaningful input is provided and how deeply do the learners need to process it? How much of the time spent doing the activity is likely to optimize learning as opposed to being time-wasting 'busy' work, or time spent on classroom organization, or simply hanging around waiting?

Introduction

3 **Interest:** Is the activity interesting, challenging, enjoyable? How much participation and/or interaction does it involve? Is it intrinsically motivating and likely to engage participants?

4 **Versatility/adaptability:** Can the activity be applied in a wide range of contexts (such as EFL, ESL, large classes, multilingual groups, online classes, etc.)? Does it lend itself to being adapted to different contexts, to different levels of proficiency and for different purposes?

5 **Simplicity:** How easy is the activity to set up and moderate? How much preparation and material support does it require? How economical is it in terms of the time needed to set it up in relation to the time spent on task?

6 **Spin-off:** Does the activity have beneficial consequences beyond immediate language learning, in terms – for example – of developing learner autonomy, enhancing motivation, or building a positive classroom climate?

7 **Validation:** How grounded is the activity in theories of learning and, specifically, second language learning? Is there any research that supports the use of such an activity? Is there evidence – even anecdotal – that the activity has positive learning outcomes?

How to use this book

The activities have been grouped into six categories: the four skills (*Speaking, Listening, Writing, Reading*) plus the two main language systems: *Grammar* and *Vocabulary.* These reflect the way many teaching and training curricula are divided up. Nevertheless, many – if not most – of the activities involve a combination of skills and systems. 'Running dictation' (page 121), for example, involves reading, speaking, listening and writing, and the final product integrates grammar and vocabulary. For ease of access, however, we have assigned activities to the categories that best reflect the skill or system that is either the dominant focus during the activity, or the final product. In the case of 'Running dictation', this is writing. Further information as to which activities are appropriate for specific teaching contexts (e.g. teaching business English, or teaching young learners) can be found in the *Index* at the back of the book.

Basic information, including an outline of the activity, the level of students and the preparation that is needed, is provided in the text. The authors' own comments on the activity – where available – are also included, along with an editorial comment which typically underscores each activity's potential, including ways that it might be adapted, and different subskills that it might activate.

Perhaps some of the activities in this book will already be familiar to you. So a first stage might be to browse through and note ones that are new but inviting: ones that trigger the response 'Wow, good idea, hadn't thought of that, would like to try it out!'

Then there's the issue of when and where to implement them. One danger of a focus on language learning activities in isolation is that it might encourage the view that language teaching is simply the stringing together of randomly-chosen activities, with little thought given to the overall coherence of the lesson or scheme of work. Hence, a key criterion in selecting an activity is its 'fit', i.e. how appropriate the activity is in terms of your immediate, mid-term or long-term teaching goals. 'Fit' is not an absolute quality: it can be assessed only in relation to the learning and teaching context, including the syllabus, coursebook, assessments and, importantly, the learners' needs

100 Great Activities: The Best of the Cambridge Handbooks for Language Teachers

and dispositions. An activity 'fits' when it supports the broader curricular goals – if, for example, it provides reinforcement of a pre-selected grammar item; if it's an engaging way of reviewing previously taught vocabulary; if it generates interest in the topic of the immediate coursebook unit; if it raises awareness about useful learning skills and strategies, and so on.

You shouldn't feel that you need to do the activity exactly the way it's laid out here. One of our criteria for a good activity is its flexibility (see point 4 above): it can be done in different ways and invites variation. If you feel that the basic idea is a good one, think of how you could introduce different ways of doing it, or of extending it or, conversely, ways to shorten or streamline it, that would suit your students and your own teaching style and teaching context. You will probably use the activity more than once: each time you'll reflect and learn something from what went well, or from what went not so well, or from feedback from students. If you are working in a team, share the activities with other teachers: you may well find that they have more ideas to add!

Accordingly, we invite you to browse, choose, decide where and when you can use the ideas, adapt, implement, reflect, share – and enjoy!

Reference

Du Plessis, A. (2013) *Cambridge English Language Teaching Publishing 1973–1988: A personal history.* Cambridge University Press.

1 Speaking

It probably won't surprise you that the largest section in this book is devoted to activities whose primary focus is on speaking. After all, the goal for most learners is to achieve a degree of spoken fluency. And yet many students are reluctant – through lack of confidence or shyness – to speak in the target language in the classroom. Of course, speaking never occurs in a vacuum, and most of the activities in this section are designed to maximize opportunities for two-way interaction and provide an incentive for resolving communication breakdowns.

One way of doing this is to incorporate an 'information gap': I have some information – you have to find it out. 'Describe and draw' is a classic example of this principle. The information gap is also the basis of many game-type activities of the 'Guess what animal I am' type, but also activities designed to build a warm and supportive classroom dynamic through the sharing of personal information, as in 'What do we have in common?'

There are other activities in this section that focus on specific subskills of speaking, including pronunciation ('Pronouncing places, products and planets', 'Chants') and question formation ('Interview interrogatives'), while still others encourage longer speaking turns, such as '30-second stimulus talks' and 'Recorded stories'.

100 Great Activities: The Best of the Cambridge Handbooks for Language Teachers

1.1 30-second stimulus talks

From *Language Activities for Teenagers* edited by Seth Lindstromberg

Outline	Students give very brief oral presentations
Author's comment	This short oral fluency exercise is easy to set up and run in classes ranging from low-intermediate to advanced proficiency. It could be called 'A gentle, shallow-end-of-the-pool introduction to giving oral presentations'. Tessa Woodward – who created the activity – describes how this exercise can be a regular feature of lessons and how it can provide a basis for students to give talks that increase in length and that involve increasing participation by listeners.
Editors' comment	As an alternative or follow-up to the procedure suggested here, presentations can be recorded digitally, either just audio or also video. Students can use simple texting tools such as WhatsApp, or more advanced ones based on tools such as ScreenPal. Either way, recording is less stressful than speaking in class, and gives the students the possibility of deleting and redoing their presentation if they feel they can do better.
Level	Pre-intermediate to Advanced (B1–C1)
Preparation	Decide what object of yours you are going to talk about at stage 4.

Procedure

1   Explain that everyone will be giving one or more very short talks about an object.

2   Offer them a few opening and closing phrases such as:

   I'm going to talk about . . . or *I've decided to talk about . . .* or
   I've brought with me . . . and *That's it* or *That's all I want to say.*

3   Teach some easy audience questions such as:

   Can you tell me more about . . . ?

4   Give a very short talk yourself, one of no more than 30 seconds, and speak very slowly.
   For example:

   I've decided to talk to you about my bicycle bell. I've brought it in so you can see it. It's very old. I like the sound it makes. I never clean it. That's it.

5   The prime aim here is not to give a really interesting talk about your object but rather to show your students that talking about an object is easy.

6   Ask students to bring in photos, objects, talismans, mascot toys and so on.

7   In later lessons, invite one or more students who have brought something in to sit at the front and 'show and tell' in English.

Speaking

Variations

1 Once students have got used to speaking for 30 seconds (or whatever time you start with), make the time limit a bit longer.

2 Try to elicit more and more audience questions.

Tips

- Call students up to present when there is a good, relaxed atmosphere in class.
- If a student is still talking fluently after 30 seconds have gone by, allow them to continue. But if they do go over, as soon as they start hesitating, gently bring them to a halt by congratulating them for speaking longer than the specified time. The point of initially specifying a 30-second time limit is to make students approach the task feeling it will be relatively easy to do.

Acknowledgement
Contributed by Tessa Woodward

100 Great Activities: The Best of the Cambridge Handbooks for Language Teachers

1.2 Alibi

From *Lessons from Nothing: Activities for language teaching with limited time and resources* by Bruce Marsland

Outline	Students try to find flaws in an invented story by asking questions of three different 'suspects'
Author's comment	The small working groups in this activity are set up so that not everyone has the same objective. Some are trying to tell a story while others are trying to question the narrative. As a consequence, this activity can lead to authentic functional language use. In a virtual learning environment, the activity can be arranged by giving groups their own virtual 'rooms' to create their alibi or interrogate their suspects.
Editors' comment	This activity also provides meaningful and communicative practice of the past simple and past continuous tenses/aspects, in both question and statement form. So you might want to draw students' attention to these forms before or after the activity itself.
Level	Intermediate to Advanced (B1+–C1)
Preparation	None

Procedure

1   This game will be familiar to many teachers in some form. A crime (usually a hideous murder) is said to have been committed the previous evening between the hours of 6 and 7 o'clock. Build the tension by suggesting that three students in the class are suspected. Choose the students and name them.

2   Ask these three students to leave the classroom (or move out of earshot) and devise their 'alibis' for the hour when the crime was committed. Stress to them that they must know the exact details of what they did and where they went. Also stress that they must claim to have been together the whole time. They are not allowed to say 'I don't remember'.

3   While the three students are deciding on their story, split the rest of the class into three groups, each of which will interview each suspect in turn. If they have a pen and piece of paper, they can nominate a note-taker; otherwise the whole group will, like good detectives, have to rely on memory. Together, group members decide on some good questions to ask. They can also decide who will ask the questions, and where the suspect will sit (or stand).

4   After 5–10 minutes, bring the three suspects back into the classroom. One goes to each group for questioning, which can last for about five minutes, and then the groups swap suspects. All three groups get the chance to question all three suspects separately. Ensure that the witnesses are out of earshot of one another.

Speaking

5 Any difference between the suspects' stories will be seen as proof of guilt. Maybe not all the suspects are guilty – it is up to the interrogating groups to decide. At the end of the questioning sessions, gather the evidence from the three groups orally, and take a class vote to decide which (if any) of the students is guilty.

6 If you have any time remaining, the class may wish to decide on a suitable punishment.

Acknowledgement
This method of setting up the activity comes from:
Ur, P. (1981) *Discussions that Work: Task-centred fluency practice*. Cambridge University Press.

100 Great Activities: The Best of the Cambridge Handbooks for Language Teachers

1.3 All-purpose needs check

From *Teach Business English* by Sylvie Donna

Outline	Students share their learning needs and expectations for a course or lesson
Author's comment	A simple activity, conceptually, but useful to check needs for any type of student – even young learners or exam students. It should increase students' interest and increase learning, as students will have chosen what the primary focus is in that lesson or course. As you will see, it can be done with zero technology or using apps and a full virtual learning environment (VLE) or Microsoft Teams messages or whatever – depending on your circumstances and preference. This procedure can be used on courses based on set materials and in cases where a range of resources are used, or are created by the teacher for a specific group or class type.
Editors' comment	This may be used very early on in the course, maybe even during the first meeting, in order to help plan content and establish priorities. Not only will it help plan the course and, as the author says, increase student motivation, but it also conveys an important message: that the teacher respects and will pay attention to the expressed needs of members of the class.
Level	Elementary to Advanced (A2–C1)
Preparation	None

Procedure

1 Explain to students that you would like to confirm (or identify) their precise needs so as to make the course (or lesson) as useful to them as possible.

2 Next, draw two intersecting lines on the board, and write the words 'Speaking', 'Listening', 'Writing' and 'Reading' in the four quadrants (see example below), or other headings, depending on the nature of the course or class.

3 Ask for a volunteer student to write suggestions on the board in the appropriate quadrant; encourage them to invite another student to take control after a while, and continue to do this so that various students lead the activity. Note that other areas or columns may be added if a suggestion does not fit any of the quadrants.

4 Ask students to call things out for the volunteer to write down. Don't correct students' language as they speak, as the focus is communication.

5 When each quadrant has a list of items (however long or short), tell students that they are now going to check how many students in the group need to focus on each area. Ask them to raise their hands to vote for the main items they need as you call them out.

6 Discuss the results, and if doing this activity for a whole course, tell students that you will prepare or adapt a course outline which reflects the decisions made. Distribute this course outline in the next lesson. Be aware that you may need to remind students of the advertised or funded focus of a course, or urgent exam-related needs.

Example quadrant

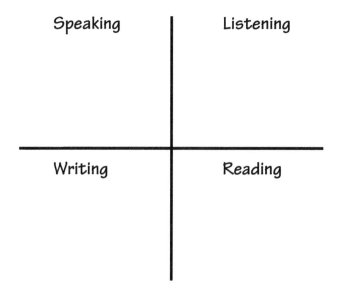

Follow-up
So that you can keep your needs analysis up-to-date, encourage students to message you on an ongoing basis with any other thoughts or requests.

Variation
1 If you're teaching online (or even face to face), consider using a digital noticeboard app such as Padlet (using columns, rather than quadrants) to get students listing their perceived needs. This can either be done live or on an ongoing basis. In both cases a Padlet (or other app) can easily be embedded within your virtual learning environment, if you have one.
2 You might want to give students lists of items under headings to discuss and vote on. This can easily be done with a handout, with one student noting down the tallies for each item, or even more easily using a voting app such as Poll Everywhere or Mentimeter.

100 Great Activities: The Best of the Cambridge Handbooks for Language Teachers

1.4 Becoming a picture

From *Drama Techniques: A resource book of communication activities for language teachers 3rd edition* by Alan Maley and Alan Duff

Outline	Students imagine themselves as someone else as shown in a picture, and describe their situation and sensations
Authors' comment	The devil is in the detail! The more specific and detailed students' description and interpretation is, the more convincing their new personality will be.
Editors' comment	This could be done just imagining details about the person in the picture, but is far more powerful if the students are asked to identify with them and speak or write in the first person. The notes that they take at stage 2 of the activity could be extended to a whole essay, or formatted as a CV or a personal website, either of which would be illustrated by the original picture.
Level	Elementary to Upper Intermediate (A2–B2)
Preparation	You need enough pictures for one per student. The pictures should show the portrait of someone interesting to look at. Avoid portraits of well-known people. The pictures could be on paper or displayed on students' digital devices.

Procedure

1   Students work individually. Give each one a portrait, or send a digital version to their smartphones or other digital devices.

2   Tell them that they are going to 'become' this person. Then allow 20 minutes for them to flesh out their new personality. They should make notes to remind themselves of their interpretation. Display the guidelines below on the board to help focus their thinking.

3   Each student joins with a partner. They show each other their pictures. Then they introduce themselves as the person in the picture. When they have finished, the partners can ask supplementary questions and make comments.

4   Ask for a volunteer, or nominate one student, who will be interviewed by the whole class. The student must reply to all the questions in role.

Follow-up
In the next class, students work in groups of four, and use their pictures/characterisations to develop a dramatized sketch involving all four characters.

Speaking

Guidelines

The world outside the frame of the picture:
- Where was this picture taken? What can be seen outside the frame?
- What things are near? Far?
- What sort of place is this? How does it look, sound, smell?
- Are there other people nearby? What do people do here?
- Why are you (i.e. the person in the portrait) there?

The person:
- Name, age, where born (city, country), family?
- Where do you live?
- Occupation/career?
- What are you most proud of in your life?
- What do you enjoy doing most?
- How would you describe your usual appearance?
- How would you describe your personality?
- What do you hate most?
- When you leave this place, where will you go? What will you do next?
- What kinds of food do you like?
- What kind of clothes do you wear?
- How do you walk, sit, stand? What does your voice sound like?

1.5 Chants

From *Discussions and More: Oral fluency practice in the classroom* by Penny Ur

Outline	Students learn by heart and recite chants based on natural utterances
Author's comment	It was Carolyn Graham who introduced and popularized *Jazz Chants* – have a look at her YouTube recordings, or read any of her books – and my adaptation here is based on her ideas. Students recite rhythmic chants that replicate the rhythm of natural speech and have an enjoyable 'beat', rather like rap music. Students love them, and the chunks of English that they learn from reciting them remain with them forever.
Editors' comment	Chants are not only a great way of practising the rhythms of speech (even if exaggerated). They also provide a fun context for incorporating useful 'chunks' of language – formulaic expressions such as greetings, or useful classroom language – and the built-in repetition ensures memorization.
Level	Beginner to Elementary (A1–A2)
Preparation	Select a chant, such as one of those shown below, or compose your own.

Procedure

1   Perform the chant you have chosen, emphasizing the strong beats (in capital letters) with finger clicks or claps. In the following example, the rows of dots indicate a 'rest' or pause for a beat:

HI ... LOU ... HOW are YOU?
HI ... LOU ... HOW are YOU?
HI ... KATE, i'm FEEling GREAT
and HOW ... ARE ... YOU?

2   Begin by asking students to repeat just the first line after you, two or three times.

3   Continue, gradually adding more lines until they can say the whole chant by heart.

4   Encourage them to add gestures: for example, shaking hands with a partner when they say 'Hi', pointing to the partner at 'How are you?' and to themselves at 'I'm feeling great.' The dialogue can later be performed by pairs of students, each one taking a different role (Kate/Lou).

5   In the next lesson, ask the class to recall and recite the whole chant.

Follow-up

1   In later lessons, ask students to perform the chant in small groups or in pairs, dividing the lines between them so that the chant comes out as a conversational exchange (but maintaining the rhythm).

2   Afterwards, suggest that they recite the chant, either in chorus or individually, varying the tempo, volume and voice pitch: for example, performing it very slowly or quickly; loudly or softly; with a crescendo or diminuendo; at a high or low pitch.

Speaking

Variations

1 With classes who can read fluently, write up the chant on the board at the beginning. Erase segments as they are learnt by heart so that by the end you have erased the whole chant and students can recite from memory.

2 Chants can be used to practise specific language points, such as grammar or vocabulary. See, for example, the last two samples below for chants that practise forms of the present simple.

Samples

1 WHAT? . . . WHAT? i DON'T understand . . . (× 2)
please SAY it AGAIN (× 3)
[CLAP . . . CLAP]

---

2 ENGlish, ARabic, FRENCH . . . (× 2)
ENGlish, ARabic (× 2)
ENGlish, ARabic, FRENCH.
(or substitute any sequence of words with 2, 3 and 1 syllables)

---

3 DO you like DANcing? YES i DO . . . (× 2)
HE likes DANcing, HE likes DANcing!
I like DANcing TOO!
DO you like FOOTball? YES, i DO . . . ! (× 2)
SHE likes FOOTball, SHE likes FOOTball!
I like FOOTball TOO!

---

4 he DOESn't like DEAN . . . NO? why NOT . . . ? (× 2)
he DOESn't like DEAN beCAUSE he's MEAN,
but HE likes DOT, a LOT!
she DOESn't like LILLy . . . NO? why NOT . . . ? (× 2)
she DOESn't like LILLy beCAUSE she's SILLY,
but SHE likes DOT, a LOT!

From *100 Great Activities* © Cambridge University Press and Assessment 2024   PHOTOCOPIABLE

100 Great Activities: The Best of the Cambridge Handbooks for Language Teachers

1.6 Congratulations

From *Personalizing Language Learning* by Griff Griffiths and Kathy Keohane

Outline	Students congratulate each other
Editors' comment	This can be used as an ice-breaker early in the course; it also teaches a useful set of congratulatory expressions. You might also add ways of acknowledging congratulations: 'Thank you!', 'That's so kind of you', etc. A further extension is to get students to continue to talk after the initial congratulation and acknowledgement, asking for and giving more details of the happy event.
Level	Elementary to Upper Intermediate (A2–B2)
Preparation	Have available large sticky labels, or pieces of paper with pins.

Procedure

1   Ask learners to think of the nicest thing that has happened to them recently. Then ask them to write it on a sticky label or piece of paper.

2   Brainstorm many ways of congratulating people and expressing pleasure. Add your own if the list is too sparse.

3   Ask learners to display their happy event by sticking or pinning it on themselves.

4   Then they circulate, shaking hands and expressing their pleasure at each other's good fortune until all have congratulated and been congratulated. The following are some examples of language you might expect to hear:

Brilliant! I'm really pleased you've got a part in the school play.
Well done – I'm delighted to hear you drove on the motorway for the first time.
Congratulations! I'm so happy your rabbit is well again.
Fantastic! It's so nice to know you won a prize at the weekend.

Variation

1   Pair learners. Ask them to think of a recent personal achievement. The activity works best if learners choose something very simple, such as 'I managed not to mislay my glasses all week.' They should write this down and give it, or send it as a text message, to their partner.

2   Now suggest they write a short message congratulating their partner on this achievement. The message should be as complimentary as possible. For example:

Dear Zuhair

I was so pleased to hear that you managed not to mislay your glasses all week. It's so easy to just put them down and forget about them, but you didn't do that! You should be really proud of yourself for managing to find them whenever you wanted them. Well done indeed!

Best wishes
Hanna

---

3   Finally, learners give, or send as a text message, their written congratulations to their partners.

Speaking

1.7 Course evaluation

From *Ways of Doing: Students explore their everyday and classroom processes* by Paul Davis, Barbara Garside and Mario Rinvolucri

Outline	Students brainstorm aspects of the course that could be changed or improved
Authors' comment	Barbara Garside: This is a versatile and interactive way to manage feedback at the end of any course, training session or conference. Framing it as a role play can create some distance between the participants and any difficult feelings they may have. Asking them to consider future courses may give them a sense of ownership and help them see their feedback in a more positive light.
Editors' comment	Penny uses an activity like this halfway through the course (i.e. not at the end), and then uses the results to help improve the present course as it goes on, as well as to plan the next one. It's a good idea also to add a final feedback stage, where you thank the students for their input and note any comments that were particularly interesting or useful from your point of view.
Level	Intermediate to Advanced (B1+–C1)
Preparation	None

Procedure

1 Brainstorm with the whole group possible headings for aspects of the course (e.g. coursebook, supplementary materials, homework) and put these up on the board.

2 Divide the students into groups of three or four. Tell them that they are a Planning Committee for the next course, and that they must discuss how they would change or improve the course and make notes under the headings they have brainstormed. Each group should consider one aspect in detail or cover all aspects more generally.

3 Students form new groups to compare their conclusions.

4 Students give you feedback on their conclusions: orally, as a group discussion, or on the board, or on posters which are put up around the room.

Variation
Giving students in groups a blank timetable to fill in often helps them to focus on the course planning task.

1.8 Describe and draw

From *Pictures for Language Learning* by Andrew Wright

Outline	Students describe pictures to partners who have to try to draw the picture according to the description
Author's comment	It's good to get students to draw things themselves! And the speaking is based on the need to convey information helpfully and clearly. There is then physical evidence of students' success (or failure) in communicating.
Editors' comment	Penny has used this lots of times, it works beautifully. A variation she adds is that both partners have either a blank sheet of paper or a very basic sketch like the one shown here, and then take turns adding bits or colours and telling their partner to add the same (without peeping at each other's paper!). Then they check at the end to see if they have similar pictures. Another variation is for students to tell you, as the teacher (or one of the other students), what to draw on the board, and then what to add or change, or colour.
Level	Beginner to Intermediate (A1–B1+)
Preparation	A picture with some easily-described details, such as A below. Alternatively (see Variation), two pictures, one of which has details which are missing in the other (A and B below).

Procedure

1 One student has a picture (like A below, for example), a map or a plan, but does not show it to his or her partner.

2 He or she tries to describe it so that the other student can make an accurate drawing of it.

3 The 'artist' can ask questions and both must work together to make the drawing as accurate as possible.

Variation
The 'artist' is given a very basic drawing (like B above), plan or diagram which he or she must complete according to instructions given by his or her partner who has a more detailed version (like A above). The basic drawing with things missing in it can easily be made by deleting parts of the original drawing with a white-out pen, or online using a 'markup' pen coloured white in a picture file (.jpg or similar).

Speaking

1.9 Dialogue interpretation

From *Drama Techniques: A resource book of communication activities for language teachers 3rd edition* by Alan Maley and Alan Duff

Outline	Students interpret a dialogue and perform it
Authors' comment	Alan Maley: In this activity, the dialogue acts both as a mini-script and as a starting point for a scenario. Unlike many textbook dialogues, which are, if anything, over-explicit, these dialogues leave ample room for students to exercise their creative imagination.
Editors' comment	This is based on an earlier book by Maley and Duff called *Variations on a Theme*, sadly out of print today, which presented enigmatic dialogues for interpretation. You can make up your own by taking extracts from screenplays or plays whose copyright has expired, and simplifying or editing them to take out specific names or detailed information.
Level	Pre-intermediate to Upper Intermediate (B1–B2)
Preparation	You will need a number of short dialogues open to various interpretations – enough copies for one between two. Below are some examples.

Procedure

1 Students work in pairs. Distribute the same dialogue to all pairs. Explain that they have to set their dialogue in a specific context. They will need to decide who is speaking, where they are, what the topic is, what exactly is going on. Allow ten minutes for this.

2 In a whole-class session, collect ideas from students arising from their discussion.

3 Allow another ten minutes for pairs to rehearse their dialogues. Partners should take turns at reading A and B so that they each get the feel for the speaker. Finally, they perform their dialogues for the whole class.

4 Either in class, if there is time, or as homework, students should extend the dialogues into a slightly longer script, by adding a couple of lines at the beginning and some concluding lines. Encourage them to add stage directions, to give A and B names, etc.

Variation

Instead of giving the same dialogue to each pair, give out different ones to each pair, matching the difficulty level with the students' proficiency.

100 Great Activities: The Best of the Cambridge Handbooks for Language Teachers

Sample dialogues

Pre-intermediate

1 A: Can you see them?
  B: No, where are they?
  A: Look, over there, behind that tree.
  B: Wow! That's really interesting!

2 A: How long?
  B: I'm not sure . . .
  A: But I need to know.
  B: Come back later then.

3 A: Please tell me.
  B: What can I tell you?
  A: You know what I mean.
  B: How CAN I tell you that?

4 A: Who did this?
  B: I'm not sure.
  A: But you must know. You were here all the time.
  B: I'm sorry . . . I can't . . . It's a secret.

Intermediate / Upper Intermediate

1 A: It's time.
  B: What do you mean?
  A: I think you know what I mean.
  B: Oh no. Not yet, surely. It can't be.
  A: Come on now.

2 A: Well, after that, what more could I say?
  B: Mm. I can see it must have been difficult for you.
  A: Difficult!

3 A: As much as that? But was it worth it?
  B: Well, you know him as well as I do. Once he's made up his mind . . .
  A: Let's just hope he doesn't live to regret it.

4 A: Will it be enough, do you think?
  B: When is it ever enough?
  A: Yes. I wonder if they'll ever be satisfied.

From *100* *Great Activities* © Cambridge University Press and Assessment 2024   PHOTOCOPIABLE

Speaking

1.10 Discussion group tag

From *Off the Page: Activities to bring lessons alive and enhance learning* by Craig Thaine

Outline	Students discuss a topic in groups. At different times during the discussion, one student from each group moves to another group
Author's comment	This is a very simple and easy-to-set-up activity for discussions. Not only does it generate more spoken language but it also enhances classroom dynamics by varying group interactions. It is an activity that can be used with a wide range of levels and learning contexts. It is also suitable for online teaching as students can move around different breakout rooms.
Editors' comment	Classroom discussions tend to run out of steam quite quickly, but the idea of constantly 'refreshing' groups is a great way to keep a discussion going. It also ensures that all students speak, as the new participant will always need to report on what was said in his or her previous group.
Level	Elementary to Advanced (A2–C1)
Preparation	It is not necessary to prepare any materials for this activity, but it is a good idea to plan the groups and the way you will get students to move from one group to another.

Procedure

1 Provide a topic or task to discuss in groups, and write it on the board.

2 Students do any preparatory work for the discussion. For example, they can think about the topic and makes notes on what they want to say.

3 Put students in groups of four to six. Arrange the groups in the room so there is a clear sense of clockwise or anticlockwise movement. Give each student a number in their group. (Teach the words *clockwise* and *anticlockwise* if students don't know them already.)

4 Start the discussion, and when you call a number and direction, the students with that number move either clockwise or anticlockwise, e.g. *Student three – clockwise.*

5 Students find out from the new group member what the other group was talking about and then continue their discussion.

6 Repeat the procedure every two or three minutes or when you sense discussion is lagging in a group.

7 For feedback, ask students what difference it made when a new group member arrived.

Note and variation

In this activity, a lot of extra speaking is generated when the student who is new to the group reports on what his or her previous group has been saying about the topic. With a smaller class where there are only two or three groups, you could just move students by monitoring, choosing a student and letting them know which group to move to. This approach means the mixing of students can be more targeted in terms of students' strengths and weaknesses.

100 Great Activities: The Best of the Cambridge Handbooks for Language Teachers

1.11 Find someone who

From *Keep Talking: Communicative fluency activities for language teaching* by Friederike Klippel

Outline	Students talk to each other in order to find classmates who accord with 'find someone who' qualities from a list
Author's comment	This activity works both as a warming-up exercise in a new group and a useful priming situation before working on a new topic, if the prompts are chosen accordingly. Thus, e.g. elementary learners might find out about each other's pets and hobbies, a group of language teachers could tap into each other's teaching experience and tips, and students of English could find out about the linguistic and cultural knowledge their co-students possess.
Editors' comment	Two nice things about this one: it activates all the members of the class simultaneously, so nobody is bored or left out. Also, the handout provides useful scaffolding: students don't have to invent their utterances, they can base them on the written text, but use them purposefully to elicit responses. You might find it useful to run through in advance all the items that appear on their handout to make sure everyone understands them.
Level	Elementary to Upper Intermediate (A2–B2)
Preparation	Select items you want to use from the list below, or adapt, or invent your own, copy and distribute to students as a handout. There should be at least half as many items as there are students in the group.

Procedure

1 Each student receives a handout.

2 Everyone walks around the room and questions other people about things on the handout.

3 As soon as somebody finds another student who answers 'yes' to one of the questions, they write his or her name in the appropriate space and go on to question someone else, because each name may only be used once. (If a student overhears somebody answering 'yes' to another person's question they are not allowed to use that name themselves.)

4 After a given time (e.g. 15 minutes) or when someone has filled in all the blanks, the questioning stops.

5 Students read out what they have found out. They can preface their report with their own response, for example: 'I was surprised that X liked . . .'.

Speaking

Find someone who . . .

likes doing sudoku..

is not using WhatsApp...

reads more than one book in two weeks..

chews chewing gum...

has been to Africa...

can recite the alphabet in under 10 seconds...

owns a pet with four legs..

has more than three brothers or sisters...

is wearing something white...

has played this game before..

has a driving licence..

likes liquorice...

knows what lads and lasses are...

can whistle popular tunes..

collects something interesting...

can tell you a joke in English...

has an e-bike or a scooter..

has never eaten pizza...

was born on a Sunday..

has flown in a helicopter or a glider...

can speak other languages apart from English and their own language.................................

is optimistic about the future..

thinks recycling is important...

has never had a broken arm or leg..

likes rain...

keeps fit by jogging regularly..

From *100 Great Activities* © Cambridge University Press and Assessment 2024   PHOTOCOPIABLE

1.12 Flashing

From *Five-Minute Activities: A resource book of short activities* by Penny Ur and Andrew Wright

Outline	Students try to identify the content of a picture they only see for a moment
Authors' comment	Another possibility using a projector, or the 'share screen' if you are teaching through videoconferencing, is to display a bit of a picture, or a picture out of focus. Then gradually reveal the whole picture, or reduce the fuzziness, encouraging guesses as you go.
Editors' comment	Another variant on this is to choose a picture story of about four frames, cut it up into its individual frames and enlarge these; divide the class into four groups (or as many groups as there are frames in the narrative) and then flash one of the frames, in random order, to each group – one frame per group. In their groups they have to reconstruct what they saw, and then the students are re-grouped so that the new groups comprise a member of each of the original groups; they then tell each other what they 'saw' and together they try to reconstruct the sequence of the narrative. This works particularly well for pictures of accidents, because it reflects what often happens when various witnesses have to share memories of what they saw.
Level	Beginner to Intermediate (A1–B1+)
Preparation	Have ready pictures, texts or other simple displays to show on the screen or on paper.

Procedure

You can flash any of the following for a brief moment: a picture; a text; a newspaper headline. You can either do this using paper, as shown in the sketch below (but then mount it on card to make the flashing easier); or project it for a moment onto the board or screen. Or you could use an object (fishing it out of a bag for a brief moment). The students then identify and/or describe what they saw. Encourage differences of opinion and do not confirm or reject any ideas. Flash several times to promote attempts at identification and discussion. In the end, show the text, picture or object.

Little finger and thumb against the ⟶ back of the picture

Speaking

1.13 Getting students to ask the questions

From *Classroom Management Techniques* by Jim Scrivener

Outline	Students prepare questions about a topic
Author's comment	In most classes, it's the teacher who asks the vast majority of questions. Why not turn this around and get students to ask questions? It can make for a surprisingly exciting activity and builds a positive sense of students being in (at least partial) control of things.
Editors' comment	Scott recalls: when I was a very new teacher, a class of mine was observed by my supervisor who said, after it was over, 'It was a very nice lesson. But who was asking all the questions?' That one question changed my teaching forever! This activity is a simple but effective way of reversing the interactional flow.
Level	Any
Preparation	None

Procedure

1 One simple idea is to hold a question and answer session on something that you have just been studying (e.g. a reading text or a language point) or a general interest topic (e.g. the latest talent show series on TV). Ask the students to prepare (as pairs or in groups) a list of questions they would like to ask you. They can be any kind: factual questions, curiosity questions and so on.

2 Monitor and help students word the questions well.

3 When they are ready, sit at the front and let them ask you. Keep your answers brief and interesting. Remember that the focus is on their questions more than your answers.

4 After each response from you, invite follow-on questions to explore the subject a little more.

100 Great Activities: The Best of the Cambridge Handbooks for Language Teachers

1.14 Guess the animal in 20 questions

From *Five-Minute Activities for Young Learners* by Penny McKay and Jenni Guse

Outline	Students ask *yes/no* questions to guess the mystery animal
Authors' comment	This offers a fun way to integrate language goals. For grammar, students practise basic structures for *yes/no* questions and present tense verbs. For vocabulary, they revisit names of animals; the animal's environment, e.g. water; and verbs describing the animal's actions, e.g. fly. The questioner requires accurate and clear pronunciation, and the student at the front has to be able to listen carefully to the question. Guessing foods, places and people could be substituted for animals.
Editors' comment	A classic guessing game that ticks all the 'communicative' boxes: it is interactive, it requires listening as well as speaking, and it is goal-oriented. It is a fun variation of the more adult version: 'Guess my job.' Of course, you can use the same procedure for any category of items, not just animals (as mentioned by the authors above): objects, professions, places, colours, sports, etc.
Level	Elementary to Intermediate (A2–B1+)
Preparation	None

Procedure

1   Model the activity by thinking of an animal, and ask the children to ask questions to guess what it is (see example below). Elicit *yes/no* questions and write these on the board. You can decide if you want to use 'it' questions (*Can it fly?*) or 'you' questions (*Can you fly?*) but you should keep the pronoun consistent.

2   Choose a child to come to the front of the class. This child decides on an animal. Check that it is a suitable choice for the game.

3   The rest of the class asks questions in order to guess the animal.

4   Whoever guesses the animal has the next turn. If nobody can guess in 20 questions, then the child at the front of the class wins a point.

Example questions about animals

Sample questions	Sentence stems
1 Do you live near water?	Do you live . . . ?
2 Do you eat grass?	Do you eat . . . ?
3 Do you give milk to your babies?	Do you give . . . ?
4 Can you fly?	Do you have . . . ?
5 Can you swim?	Can you . . . ?
	Are you . . . ?

26

Speaking

1.15 How do they rank?

From *Teaching Adult Second Language Learners* by Heather McKay and Abigail Tom

Outline	Students rank jobs according to given criteria
Authors' comment	This basic activity can be adapted to a variety of topics, such as energy sources, pets, means of communication, inventions, places to visit, with criteria as well as topics proposed by the students. Even if the class seems homogeneous, re-grouping the students for a second round is still productive.
Editors' comment	This activity is designed for adults, but can be adapted to any age group. Note that participants are very likely to use the comparative and superlative of adjectives as they discuss the issues, so the activity is a nice way of practising this grammar communicatively.
Level	Elementary to Advanced (A2–C1)
Preparation	None

Procedure

1   Ask the class to brainstorm a list of ten jobs.

2   Then ask each student to rank the jobs according to each of the following criteria. In each case, 1 will be the lowest rank and 10 will be the highest.
   - Status
   - Pay
   - Level of education
   - Appeal

3   Divide the class into groups. The group then tries to come to a definitive ranking according to their views.

4   Re-group the students and have them compare and discuss their rankings.

5   Have the groups report back to the whole class anything that surprised, or that particularly interested, them in the discussion.

100 Great Activities: The Best of the Cambridge Handbooks for Language Teachers

1.16 Interview interrogatives

From *Teach Business English* by Sylvie Donna

Outline	Students plan questions for a job interview, perform the interview, then report back to each other
Author's comment	This is a structured approach to getting students talking and reporting back on each other. It can be heavily teacher-led or more student-guided, particularly if pairs or groups of students dream up different vacancies, and if students make and evaluate recordings of their interviews on their own mobile devices. In either case it is important for the teacher to focus on accuracy when students are preparing their interview prompts.
Editors' comment	A variation on this is to divide the class into groups of three or four students. Each group decides on a position that a candidate will be applying for and designs (and notes down) questions. Then one member of each group goes to another group to be interviewed. Each interview should take five minutes. After five minutes, the interviewee returns to their group, and someone else goes to another group to be interviewed, and so on, until each group has interviewed three or four candidates. Finally, each group decides who was the best candidate, and results are shared and discussed in the full class.
Level	Elementary to Advanced (A2–C1)
Preparation	None

Procedure

1   Explain to students that they are going to interview each other, imagining they are interviewing someone for a job. As a class, decide which position is vacant; or allow individual students to choose the job they will be interviewing for.

2   Elicit and write question words and phrases on the board, e.g.:

What, Who, What kind of, How long

Then get students – individually or in small groups – to write one question for each word or phrase suitable for a job interview (or for their own interview if they chose jobs individually). Also give the students the option of adding some questions which don't feature question words (e.g. *Do you ...*) and a maximum of two 'instruction' statements (e.g. *Tell me about a situation where ...*).

3   Monitor carefully while students are preparing their questions or instruction prompts, correcting grammar, use of vocabulary, etc.

4   Ask students to choose partners and interview each other, role-playing a job interview while using the list of questions or instruction prompts prepared for that interview. (If the students have chosen which job they are interviewing for, they need to tell the interviewee what it is.)

Next, ask students to give their partner a false name and to write up an anonymous summary of the information they have discovered. Again, monitor while students do this so as to help students write their summaries accurately.

28

Speaking

5   If the interviews are all based on the same job vacancy, get students to exchange summaries with other students and decide who would be the best person to recruit for the position. If each student has chosen a different job, tell them to get together in groups and share their interview experiences.

Note

If using the above version (or the editor's suggestion), an app such as Flipgrid can be used to give students (and you) easy access to all interviews so as to evaluate each student's performance. Both you and other students can provide feedback and encouragement to individual students.

100 Great Activities: The Best of the Cambridge Handbooks for Language Teachers

1.17 Make them say it

From *The Standby Book: Activities for the language classroom* edited by Seth Lindstromberg

Outline	Students get partners to say a particular word or phrase by asking questions that elicit it
Author's comment	This fairly short oral fluency/review exercise works in both mono- and polylingual classes and at most proficiency levels, provided that students are given appropriate words and phrases to try to elicit from each other when working in trios or, perhaps ideally, in pairs. 'Make them say it' can be used as a warm-up or as an exercise for students who finish a longer activity (such as a test) well before other students do. If to-be-elicited language is varied, this exercise can be used multiple times with the same class.
Editors' comment	Penny finds it useful to do a full-class rehearsal before beginning the pairwork. Have one student with their back to the board, write a word or phrase on the board and tell the class that they have to get the student to say the word by asking them questions to which the target word or phrase is the answer. After a couple of rounds like this, put them into pairs to do the activity as described here. An easier variation is to allow answers that are slightly different from that on the slip: for example, *When I was young* instead of *When I was a child*.
Level	Elementary to Upper Intermediate (A2–B2)
Preparation	Slips of paper, several more than the number of students in the class, each with a different word or phrase which the students know. For example: *Yesterday, No, I hate it!, Wednesday.*

Procedure

1 Put participants into pairs, A and B. Give a slip of paper to everyone, asking them to keep it secret and hidden from their partner.

2 Keep the reserve slips in a pile on your desk or in a central location accessible to all.

3 A starts by asking B questions. The questions should be carefully designed to force B to say the word/phrase on A's slip. (Remember, B does not know what this word/phrase is.) Thus, if you are teaching in the UK and 'In September' is written on A's slip, then *When does the school year start?* would be a good question for A to put to B, because B might well respond, *In September.*

4 Once B has come out with the exact words on A's slip, then A and B switch roles.

5 As pairs finish, they swap their slips with new ones from the central pile, so they have more to work on.

Variations

1 At Elementary level, I call the activity 'Question practice' and give students words/phrases like these on their slips:

No, I can't.	*In the evening.*	*Sometimes.*
Switzerland.	*Tomorrow.*	*Maybe.*

30

Speaking

This means that relatively straightforward questions get practised (e.g. *Can you speak Russian?*, *Where do you come from?*, *When do you study?*, *When is our next class?*, *Do you do homework?*, *Are you going to go on the next excursion?*).

2   At higher levels, you can script what's on the slips to encourage practice of particular tenses, functional expressions and so on. Keep a few really difficult ones up your sleeve for the people who get absolutely terrific at the activity. Here are some samples:

When I was a child.	*I wish I could.*
It depends.	*I don't think so.*
If I have time.	*No, I wouldn't.*
Yes, I would have.	*I'm sorry, I'd rather not answer that!*

These take skill and persistence to elicit. Incidentally, it's amazing what personal questions people will actually answer before they finally say, 'I'm sorry, I'd rather not answer that'!

Note
It can be helpful to discuss 'near misses' so that people know that their questions have to be finely tuned. An example of a near miss is 'Are you married?' – if you're trying to get your partner to say 'Single' – since typical answers to this question would be 'Yes' or 'No'. Better questions would be, 'What do you call a person who's not married?' Of course, you could get the answer 'Happy' or 'Carefree' – there is a joker in every class, thank goodness!

Acknowledgement
Contributed by Tessa Woodward

100 Great Activities: The Best of the Cambridge Handbooks for Language Teachers

1.18 Management tips

From *Five-Minute Activities for Business English* by Paul Emmerson and Nick Hamilton

Outline	Students suggest tips for business managers
Authors' comment	This is a simple activity which draws on learners' experience in management, and naturally tends to lead into anecdotes about where the tips come from. With mixed nationalities, it will also reveal intercultural aspects that learners enjoy exploring. The emerging language will then focus on verb and noun phrase collocations, for example 'Don't take yourself too seriously.' There are also lots of short video clips on the internet of CEOs talking about the advice they would give people starting out, or that they wish they'd been given when they started.
Editors' comment	This activity can be expanded to discussion of tips for any professional activity the students are familiar with: for example, school students can suggest tips for teachers, or for the school principal, or for incoming students in the course.
Level	Elementary to Advanced (A2–C1)
Preparation	None

Procedure

1 Ask students to write down two tips that they would give to a new manager in their company.

2 Invite students to come to the board and write up their tips. (If you divide the board into two sections with a vertical line, then two students can be writing at the same time.)

3 Students explain their ideas to the class.

Follow-up

Number the tips on the board. Tell students that they are now going to vote for the four tips that they like best, but they cannot vote for their own. Students first write their four numbers on a piece of paper, then vote in open class for each suggestion by raising hands. Write the totals on the board by each tip, then discuss with the group why the winning tip(s) won.

Speaking

1.19 Map-reading: the treasure hunt

From *Testing Spoken Language: A handbook of oral testing techniques* by Nic Underhill

Outline	One student describes a route to another who has to follow it on a map
Editors' comment	This can, of course, be done online. The map is shown on the screen using any simple software like Word or PowerPoint, and the student who is drawing uses a virtual pen to mark the route in response to the other student's explanation. The advantage of the online version is that the first route can be easily erased to enable the students to switch roles for the second round of the activity.
Level	Elementary to Intermediate (A2–B1+)
Preparation	Copies of simple maps. Street maps of real or imaginary towns can be used, or maps of rural areas. You can copy the example below and add place names suitable for your class. You might like also to mark a 'start here' arrow.

Procedure

1 One learner describes to another a pre-determined route along a map.

2 The second learner has to follow the route along their own unmarked map, either tracing it with a finger, or drawing it in pencil. The second learner can ask questions to clarify anything he or she didn't understand.

3 At the end of the description, the second learner marks the final point clearly on the map.

4 The partners then switch roles and repeat the activity.

Variations

1 To make the task easier, more street names and other reference points, such as named buildings, can be given.

2 To make the task harder when the tracer is able to interrogate the describer, small differences can be introduced between the maps, such as a slightly different name or a missing detail.

100 Great Activities: The Best of the Cambridge Handbooks for Language Teachers

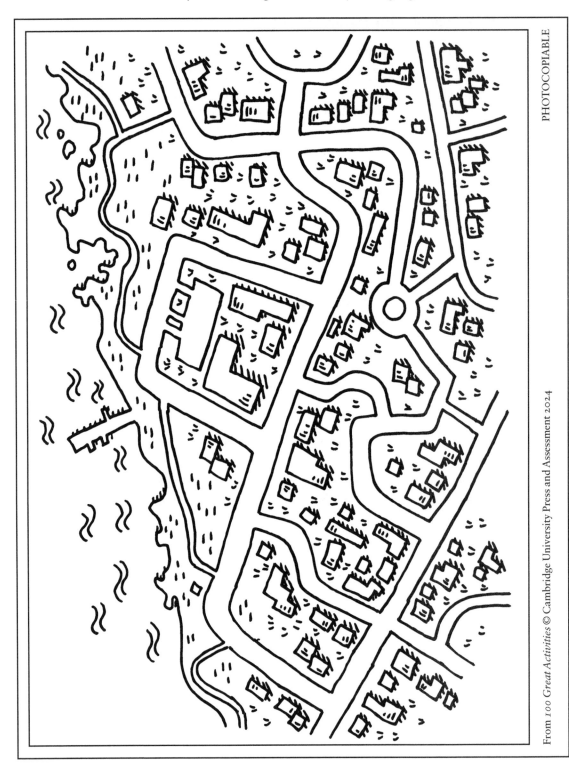

34

Speaking

1.20 Multipart story drama

From *Using Folktales* by Eric K. Taylor

Outline	Groups of students perform dramatic readings of excerpts from a folk tale
Author's comment	This activity takes a text that students have read and encourages them both to listen as other students act out their sections and to produce language themselves instead of just passively receiving it. This activity also encourages students to think about deeper aspects of meaning: what emotion the story conveys and what might be written between the lines. Finally, the active physical interpretation of the story engages more physical senses and engages different learning styles.
Editors' comment	This is a variation on the 'readers theatre' technique (check it out on the internet). Apart from the recommendations given here, suggest to your students that they can vary the text also by: using louder or softer, higher or lower voices; choral and solo reading; pause; repetition; sound effects – anything that will make it more meaningful, dramatic or entertaining for the audience. The same technique can be used, incidentally, with almost any text, for example, excerpts from coursebook reading texts.
Level	Elementary to Upper Intermediate (A2–B2)
Preparation	Choose a story with a good amount of action and preferably about three to five main characters. (With smaller classes, it is fine to have only two or three characters.) Divide the story into four or five parts. For large classes, make enough copies so that each group gets one section of the story.

Procedure

1 Divide the class into groups of three to five students and give each group one section of the story. For example, if you have 20 students and four parts, make four groups of five. If you have 60 students, form 12 groups and give each part to three groups. For some stories, you might want to have different size groups for the different parts.

2 Give students 20 minutes or so to read their section of the story together and prepare to act out their part of the story. Students may make one person a narrator if needed, and they may assign roles in any way they wish. They may also freely add dialogue to help them present the story, and they may leave out details that they don't think are essential. They may also make hasty props or use whatever they have to help them act out their part of the story. Once students have roles worked out, they should practise acting out their part.

3 Once each group has prepared its section of the story (i.e. when the time is up), call groups to the front of the class in the right order to act out their parts of the story. Other students watch until it is their group's turn to perform. If you have more than one group preparing each part, select one to present that part to the class. Try to move from one group to the next as seamlessly as possible so the story flows smoothly.

100 Great Activities: The Best of the Cambridge Handbooks for Language Teachers

1.21 Name them

From *Discussions and More: Oral fluency practice in the classroom* by Penny Ur

Outline	Students describe and name characters in a picture
Author's comment	I designed this for children, but actually it works just as well for adolescents and adults, and can go on for as long as 15 or 20 minutes. It's also a useful way of familiarizing classes with English or internationally used first names, or English versions of names from students' L1.
Editors' comment	This is an original variation of the 'describe and choose' task, a classic communicative activity, which involves two-way communication. But here it is made more meaningful by the addition of names. A fun variation might be a picture of various superheroes, or monsters, or dinosaurs – with suitably bizarre names to match!
Level	Beginner to Intermediate (A1–B1+)
Preparation	You will need a picture showing a lot of different people, as in the example below, copied for students or displayed on students' own digital devices (but if using the latter, make sure that students know how to insert text boxes onto the picture and type in the names).

Procedure

1 Brainstorm with the students all the English names, masculine and feminine, they can think of and write them up on the board. Add more, if necessary, until you have about 30 or more listed.

2 Give one copy of the picture to each student and discuss for a minute or two what they can see in it.

3 Explain the procedure: they are going to work in pairs. Once the activity starts, they may look at and write on only their own copy of the picture, not their partner's.

4 The first student will write in a name for one of the characters on their picture and then tell their partner who the character is and what the name is (e.g. *The little girl with black hair and glasses at the front – her name is Eva*). The partner may ask questions to make sure he or she has the right character and can then write in the name on their own picture.

5 Students then switch roles – the second student will dictate a description and name for the first student to write in, and so on.

6 Put students into pairs and let them start work.

7 The procedure should continue for about ten minutes, or until students have had enough.

8 Stop them, and tell them to show each other their pictures and check that they have the same names written on the same characters.

Variations

1 With less proficient monolingual classes, it is easier to allow students to write in names from their own culture. Classes who don't yet know the Latin alphabet may write in their L1 script.

2 To increase the challenge, ask students to define an occupation for each character instead of a name.

Speaking

PHOTOCOPIABLE

From *100 Great Activities* © Cambridge University Press and Assessment 2024

37

1.22 Numbers in my life

From *Personalizing Language Learning* by Griff Griffiths and Kathy Keohane

Outline	Students suggest numbers that have particular significance for them
Editors' comment	This is a very effective ice-breaker, and can be shortened and simplified by asking for fewer numbers. Alternatively, you might eliminate the stage of writing out explanations: students just try to guess as many as they can of their partner's numbers, and where they can't, the partner simply explains. A practical tip: for the first stage of writing out numbers in squares, you might just ask students to fold a piece of A4 paper three times, and then open it out, which will give them eight rectangles delineated by the creases. (This will give eight instead of ten in the original, which is fine.)
Level	Elementary to Advanced (A2–C1)
Preparation	None

Procedure

1 In class, or for homework, ask learners to divide a sheet of paper into ten squares. Inside each square, ask them to write a number which is in some way significant to them.

2 When they have finished, on a separate piece of paper, they should write down the significance of each number, taking care to write these in a different order from the original list, and without actually writing the number. This part of the task is likely to include information such as:

house number / car number plate / age / number of rooms in their house / age when they started work / number of kilometres from home to school, etc.

3 Learners then give their number grid and their explanations of the significance of the number to a partner who uses both sets of information to find out why each number has been included by asking questions, for example:

Does your car number plate have the numbers 145 in it?
Did you meet your best friend when you were 11?

4 When everybody has finished the activity, round off by asking learners to share with the rest of the class one piece of information they learned about their partner.

Variation

A quicker version of this activity involves the teacher calling out a number and asking for anyone to volunteer information about themselves relating to that number, e.g. *Three*:

- My little girl is three
- I have three sisters
- I have three siblings
- I bought three limes at the supermarket today
- There were three people waiting for the bus with me this morning, etc.

Speaking

Follow-up

When learners have volunteered information about themselves relating to the number, other learners may ask them questions about this information. For example, if one learner has said *My little girl is three*, others may ask *What's your little girl's name?* etc.

100 Great Activities: The Best of the Cambridge Handbooks for Language Teachers

1.23 Opinion poll

From *Keep Talking: Communicative fluency activities for language teaching* by Friederike Klippel

Outline	Students design and administer questionnaires to elicit classmates' opinions on various topics
Author's comment	This is an activity which may be adapted to the ages, interests and experience present in the group of learners. The procedure shown here is just one of many possible ones. This activity provides ample opportunity for speaking and writing and involves all learners simultaneously. It can also be adapted to digital learning-teaching environments.
Editors' comment	The actual survey can be done as suggested here, by redistributing groups, but there are other possibilities. For example, you might allow students to move around freely in a 'mingle', meeting other students and answering each other's questions before reassembling in their original groups to share results. Or it can be done as homework: each student takes the questions of his/her group and asks friends and family outside the classroom, coming back the next day with results. The last possibility is perhaps best if you're working in a distance-learning situation.
Level	Pre-intermediate to Upper Intermediate (B1–B2)
Preparation	None

Procedure

1 The class is given, or decides on, a topic for the opinion poll. This could be food and eating habits, shopping, travelling, work, climate change, fun, family life, equality, current affairs, ecology, and more.

2 The class decides on six sub-topics: for example, the 'food and eating habits' topic could be divided into *breakfast, drinks, eating out, favourite foods, cooking, special diets.*

3 The class is divided into six groups, each of which gets one of the sub-topics and agrees on two or three questions they want to ask about it. Each group member prepares an interview sheet using their questions. See the example below. Everyone should fill in their own answers first.

4 The groups are rearranged so that there is at least one member from each original group in each new group. Members of the group ask the others 'their' questions, and note answers. This means that in order to fill in the interview sheet each person has to talk to everybody else in the group.

5 The original groups reassemble to organize their data. This may involve quite a lot of discussion where tables or diagrams have to be drawn.

6 Each group presents their results either in the form of a short talk or by putting up lists, tables, etc. on the wall (or via data projector), so that everybody can have a look.

7 (Optional) When everybody in the class has heard what the findings were, questions like *Was there any result that surprised you? What is the most important result? How can we act on these results?* can be asked.

40

Speaking

Example
Breakfast
What do you usually have for breakfast?

Name	Food	Drink
1 Me	cereal, toast and marmalade	orange juice, two cups of coffee
2		
3		
4		
5		
6		

Variations
1   If your class is small, you may want to use fewer than six sub-topics and then divide into fewer groups.

2   Different kinds of questions or prompts can be used: open *Wh-* questions, as in the example above, or multiple-choice; true/false; statements to agree or disagree with (very much agree/agree/don't know/disagree/very much disagree); frequency questions (always/often/sometimes/rarely/never); gapfills.

41

100 Great Activities: The Best of the Cambridge Handbooks for Language Teachers

1.24 PMI

From *Keep Talking: Communicative fluency activities for language teaching* by Friederike Klippel

Outline	Students respond to statements with points that are positive or 'plus' (P), negative or 'minus' (M) or interesting (I)
Author's comment	This activity does not just practise speaking but lateral thinking and creativity as well. It is suitable for all age groups and levels of language competence. The examples may also be chosen from current controversial topics. Or the activity may be used to prepare topics raised in the textbook or other teaching materials, or to continue working on them. The group discussions can be held online in a breakout room.
Editors' comment	The activity could be prefaced with a brainstorm of suggestions for students for changes in the school or the way subjects are taught, or any other topic that is of local interest. You could then choose one of them for students to discuss PMI points relating to it. Another possibility is to propose two or three topics simultaneously, so groups choose which of them to relate to; once they have identified their PMI points for that topic, they can progress to another.
Level	Pre-intermediate to Advanced (B1–C1)
Preparation	None

Procedure

1 The students have to think of the plus points (P), minus points (M) and interesting points (I) of an idea. The teacher gives the class an idea and then everybody works on their own for a few minutes. Possible ideas:
- A new law is passed that forbids eating in all public places.
- Every family is only allowed to have meat once a month.
- People should wear badges to show what mood they are in.
- To save energy, public buildings like post offices, stations, schools and offices are no longer heated.
- A scientist discovers a way of making gold cheaply.
- Children over 5 are given the vote.
- Planes do not work anymore. They all crash after take-off.
- Everyone has to work on a farm for six months before turning 18.
- Students are allowed to employ artificial intelligence for their school and university work.

2 Each student works with a partner and they share their ideas.

3 The ideas are discussed with the whole class.

Variations

1 After the first stage above, small groups are formed who evaluate the ideas of other students.

2 Small groups rank the points mentioned by other students.

Acknowledgement
Idea adapted from:
De Bono, E. (1994) *CoRT Thinking*. Hawker Brownlow Education.

42

Speaking

1.25 Pronouncing places, products and planets

From *Pronunciation Practice Activities* by Martin Hewings

Outline	Comparing pronunciation of words in English and students' first language
Author's comment	This simple activity focuses students' attention on differences that might occur between the pronunciation of equivalent names in English and other languages. In doing so, it can help students become aware of more general differences between the pronunciation of English and their own language(s) – different patterns of word stress, vowel sounds that occur in one language but not another, different permissible consonant clusters – and so on. Students can be encouraged to go on to use online tools allowing them to hear equivalent words spoken.
Editors' comment	This is a very useful activity, not only for pronunciation but also for vocabulary. It can be applied to other proper nouns, like personal given names that have equivalents in many languages ('John', for example). You might also use sets of words that are often cognates, the same word used (slightly adapted in pronunciation and sometimes spelling) in different languages; names of subjects of study, for example; scientific or technical terminology; words relating to digital technology. And then move on to the 'Follow-up' suggested below, which relates to cognates in general.
Level	Elementary to Upper Intermediate (A2–B2)
Preparation	Write or display on the board one of the following lists: cities/states: Paris, Moscow, Quebec, Budapest, Beijing, Seoul, Johannesburg, Edinburgh, Rio de Janeiro, Brussels, Siberia; products/companies: Coca-Cola, Microsoft, Toyota, Skoda, Ikea, Qantas, Volvo; geographical features: the Himalayas, the Urals, the Sahara Desert, the Pacific Ocean, Asia, Antarctica; the planets: Mercury, Venus, Mars, Jupiter, Saturn, Uranus, Neptune, Earth; elements: Aluminium, Arsenic, Chlorine, Helium, Hydrogen, Iodine, Neon, Radium, Uranium.

Procedure

1 Point to the list on the board. If students' mother tongue uses the Latin alphabet, ask them to write down how each of the words are written in their first language and to note any differences. Then go through them and discuss their results.

2 Say words from the list, one at a time. After each, ask students to note down whether the pronunciation in English and in their language is nearly the same, different or very different for those words written the same or similarly.

3 Ask elementary students to say the words that are different or very different in pronunciation in their first language and in English. With more advanced students, talk about the differences in pronunciation in the words and whether these reflect more general differences between English and the first language. For example, in British English Moscow is pronounced /ˈmɒskəʊ/, in German it is written Moskau and pronounced close to /ˈmɒskaʊ/ and in Spanish it is written Moscú and pronounced close to /mɒsˈku/. You might note that the vowel sound /əʊ/ is not found in German or Spanish words. You might also note that while stress is on the first syllable in

43

100 Great Activities: The Best of the Cambridge Handbooks for Language Teachers

English, it is on the second in Spanish (although this does not represent a general feature of English and Spanish). In British English (the) Himalayas is pronounced /hɪmə'leɪəz/ while in French Himalaya is pronounced close to /ɪmæ'læjæ/. Here you might note that the sound /h/ is not used in French.

Follow-up

For homework, ask students to list words from their first language that have been borrowed from English, or words in English that have been borrowed from their first language. In class, some or all students could write these words on the board and give the first language pronunciation and the English pronunciation of the borrowed word (or you may need to give this). For example, words in Japanese that have been borrowed from English include *sukebo* (skateboard), *don mai* (= don't mind = don't worry), *buruusu* (= blues, i.e. a kind of music). Talk about any differences between English and Japanese pronunciation that have led to the different spellings. In other languages, words are borrowed from English and spelt the same but with different pronunciations. For example, video is written *vídeo* in Spanish and pronounced close to /'bɪðeɪəʊ/.

44

Speaking

1.26 Recorded stories

From *Language Learning with Technology: Ideas for integrating technology in the classroom* by Graham Stanley

Outline	Collaborative storytelling using recording technology
Author's comment	A fun storytelling activity that lends itself to all levels, with the technology used as a way of allowing learners to listen to themselves and to each other.
Editors' comment	This is an original version of collaborative storytelling, more familiar as a writing activity, but here reconfigured for speaking and listening. It draws on the recording technique that is associated with CLL (Counselling Language Learning); see the variation below, which is one Scott has used to good effect in his own classes.
Level	Elementary to Advanced (A2–C1)
Preparation	You'll need one recording device (e.g. smartphone or tablet with recording app) per group of learners.

Procedure

1   Tell the learners they are going to work in groups and record a story together, but before they do so, each group has to decide what kind of story it's going to be (i.e. the genre). Help the learners by brainstorming different genres of stories. Suggestions may include:

   horror   science fiction   romance   comedy   historical   fairy tale   mystery

2   They should then decide the names of the main characters in their story and some detail about their lives (how old they are, where they come from, what they do, etc.). After this, tell the learners that they are ready to begin, and make sure they are ready to record on their digital devices.

3   Learners take turns recording the sentences. When someone in the group thinks of a sentence, that learner takes the voice recorder and says that sentence, recording themselves. Tell the learners that if they want to write down the sentence first, they can do so.

4   Also tell the learners that everybody in the group should take a turn. Ask the learners to continue until they think they have reached the end of the story.

5   Once everyone has finished, they can listen to the entire story from the beginning, and then swap the voice recorders with the other groups and listen to each of the stories. Alternatively, you can listen as a class to each of the stories.

Variation

Instead of asking learners to record a story, get them to sit in circles of around five or six, and tell them they are going to have an unscripted conversation about anything they want to talk about. When any of the learners wants to say something, ask them to put their hand up, and their line of dialogue is recorded. If learners don't know how to say something in English, they can ask the teacher beforehand, trying it out and asking the teacher to correct it before it is recorded. Once the activity is finished, play back the conversation, and ask the learners to work in pairs to transcribe it. (Or, if this seems too tedious, ask the learners to use a 'speech to text' tool, and then invite them to correct the transcription.) Show the transcription on a projector to focus on features of vocabulary or grammar.

100 Great Activities: The Best of the Cambridge Handbooks for Language Teachers

1.27 Say things about a picture

From *Discussions and More: Oral fluency practice in the classroom* by Penny Ur

Outline	Students brainstorm all the things they can think of to say about a picture
Author's comment	Describing pictures is a fairly obvious routine procedure. What makes this activity fun, and produces an enormous amount of learner talk, is the 'ticks' participants earn for each utterance, plus a time limit. This combination, plus the extra stage of trying to break their own record, turns a routine exercise into a game. Competing against themselves, incidentally, is a nice variation on standard competitions: just as much fun, and a lot less stressful.
Editors' comment	This is such a productive activity and uses pictures to great effect. It also has some very useful spin-off in terms of writing, and grammar and vocabulary reinforcement, as suggested in the follow-up suggestions and variations.
Level	Beginner to Intermediate (A1–B1+)
Preparation	You will need at least two pictures showing plenty of detail and activity, that can be displayed on the board (see the examples below). Vocabulary represented in the pictures should be appropriate to the proficiency level of the students. You will also need a watch or clock with a seconds hand, or use the stopwatch on your phone.

Procedure

1   Put students into groups of three or four and tell them to elect one of them to be the 'secretary' (but reassure them that the secretary does not have to write very much!).

2   Tell students that you will display a picture and they should say sentences about it. They can start when you say *Go* and will have two minutes. The secretary writes a tick (✓) for every sentence that is said, but does NOT write them out. The secretary can also contribute sentences.

3   Look at your watch to check the time, display one picture and say *Go*.

4   Stop the talking after exactly two minutes and ask groups how many ticks they have.

5   Repeat the procedure with another picture. Groups must try to break their previous record; if they got 15 ticks the first time, they now have to get at least 16!

Follow-up

For homework, ask students to write out at least ten sentences about one of the pictures. These can be ones they remember from the activity or ones they invent themselves.

Variations

1   For younger learners, one minute is enough.

2   Beginners can say only words or brief phrases about the picture, not complete sentences.

3   If you want to practise a particular grammatical feature, you can limit the student responses accordingly: for example, you might ask them to focus on prepositions of place, or action verbs in the present progressive, or the phrase *There is/are*.

46

Speaking

PHOTOCOPIABLE

From *100 Great Activities* © Cambridge University Press and Assessment 2024

47

100 Great Activities: The Best of the Cambridge Handbooks for Language Teachers

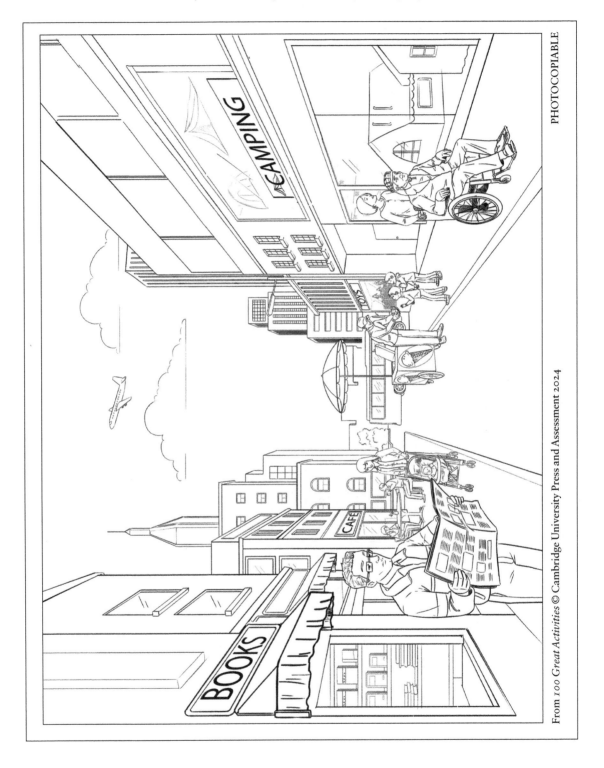

Speaking

1.28 Secret topic

From *Keep Talking: Communicative fluency activities for language teaching* by Friederike Klippel

Outline	Two students chat about something without naming it; the rest of the class try to guess what it is
Author's comment	A lot of speaking activities demand that the speakers be precise in their contributions. Therefore it seems necessary to also practise vague language (in the case of the two speakers) and – more importantly – the interpretation of vague language (in the case of the listeners) in the communicative classroom. This is a good preparation for language use in real life, e.g. in politics. In an online session, participants may offer their guesses in the chatbox, their guesses sent specifically to one of the speakers, so that the rest of the class don't see it.
Editors' comment	The first time you do this, you might demonstrate it as one of the speakers yourself, together with one of the more confident students. Later, of course, it should be members of the class: perhaps the first two who guess the secret topic the first time. To make it easier – and a bit more fun – you might suggest a code word to represent the secret topic that the two speakers are talking about: any word will do, like *coffeepot* or *jackanory*. Then whenever they want to mention the topic, they substitute the code word.
Level	Upper Intermediate to Advanced (B2–C1)
Preparation	None

Procedure

1   Two students agree on a topic they want to talk about without telling the others what it is.

2   The two students start discussing their topic without mentioning it. The others listen. Anyone in the rest of the group who thinks he or she knows what they are talking about, joins in their conversation. When about a third or half of the class have joined in, the game is stopped.

Variations

1   Students who think they know the secret topic have to write it on a piece of paper and show it to the two students before they are accepted.

2   The game can be played in teams and points awarded according to the number of people from a team who find out the secret topic.

100 Great Activities: The Best of the Cambridge Handbooks for Language Teachers

1.29 Self-directed interviews

From *Keep Talking: Communicative fluency activities for language teaching* by Friederike Klippel

Outline	Students suggest questions they would be happy to be asked in an interview
Author's comment	This activity helps to avoid embarrassment because nobody has to reveal thoughts and feelings they do not want to talk about.
Editors' comment	This is an excellent personalized and communicative practice of question forms, as well as giving opportunities for speaking. If you want to focus on particular grammatical forms, it's possible to phrase the instructions more strictly: the questions have to relate to the past or the future, for example. Or you could provide the beginning of the questions: *Have you ever . . . ? Would you like to . . . ? When did you . . . ? Why do you . . . ?*, etc.
Level	Elementary to Upper Intermediate (A2–B2)
Preparation	None

Procedure

1   Each student writes down five to ten questions that they would like to be asked. The general context of these questions can be left open, or the questions can be restricted to areas such as personal likes and dislikes, opinions, information about one's personal life, topics of recent lessons, current affairs, hobbies, etc.

2   The students choose partners, exchange question sheets and interview one another using these questions.

3   It might be quite interesting to find out in a discussion with the whole class what kinds of question were asked and why they were chosen.

Variation
Instead of fully written-up questions, each student specifies three to five topics they would like to be asked about, e.g. music, food, friends, sports.

Speaking

1.30 Speed dating

From *Dialogue Activities: Exploring spoken interaction in the language class* by Nick Bilbrough

Outline	Students find out about each other quickly through talking about chosen topics
Author's comment	Speed dating has become a popular way for people to meet potential partners. Those who participate in organized schemes are given only a few minutes to introduce themselves and to try to present their positive side. After the allotted time a bell is sounded and everyone moves round to talk to somebody else. At the end of the session they tell the organizers who it is that they would most like to meet again.
Editors' comment	This is an activity that would probably work without the time restriction, but the need to find similarities and differences while the clock is ticking adds just the right amount of urgency to the activity so that learners are pushed to the edge of their competence.
Level	Elementary to Advanced (A2–C1)
Preparation	Prepare a worksheet (see example below) on which are written a number of contrasting choices, e.g. *House or flat? Hot drinks or cold drinks? Family or friends? Meat or vegetables? Summer or spring? Cats or dogs? City or countryside? Classical or rock? Morning or evening? Meat or vegetables?*, etc. Make sure there are enough copies for each student in the class.

Procedure

1 Invite everyone to stand up in a space where they can move around fairly freely. Give out a copy of the worksheet to each student and ask them to find a partner. Tell them that one of them should choose one of the topics to discuss with their partner but that they will only have one minute to do it in. Emphasize that the interaction should be as equal as possible. Demonstrate this yourself with one student.

2 When a minute is up, give a loud signal for the end of the activity and tell them to swap partners. Each time they swap they should discuss a different topic.

3 When students have interacted with at least three other students, or when you consider it appropriate, ask everyone to sit down. Suggest that they feed back to the person they're sitting next to about who they spoke to and what they found interesting.

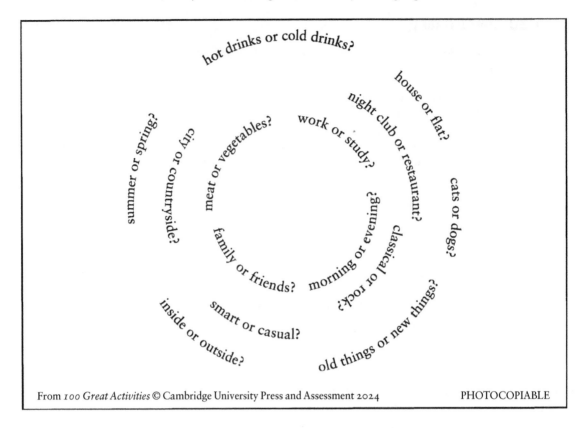

Speaking

1.31 Spoken journals

From *Language Learning with Technology: Ideas for integrating technology in the classroom* by Graham Stanley

Outline	Students keep a spoken dialogue journal, reflecting on their language learning in class
Author's comment	I've always been a fan of learner journals. Suggesting learners record their reflections can not only open up a direct channel between teachers and learners but gives learners a real opportunity to practise their speaking for homework, and the teacher's replies offer listening practice.
Editors' comment	Technology is less often associated with the speaking skill than with listening, reading and writing, but this activity exploits recording software to great effect. The fact that learners know that their spoken journals will be listened to and commented on is a huge incentive to keep re-recording until they feel they have got it right. But it's very important to discourage them from scripting the journal first, and then reading it aloud. It's easy to tell when they are doing that!
Level	Elementary to Advanced (A2–C1)
Preparation	Give your learners your email address so they can send you an audio file, and introduce them to a simple audio-recording tool: Flipgrid, for example. All of the learners need an internet-enabled computer (with a microphone) to use from home.

Procedure

1 Explain to the learners that they are going to reflect on their learning by keeping a spoken journal, and introduce them to the website you have chosen, showing them how it works by making a short recording and playing it back.

2 Hand out some questions you would like them to answer. The questions could be about what you have done in class or about their experience of learning the language. Invite them to ask you questions, too. Here are some examples:

- *What things did you find useful / did you like doing in class today?*
- *What things didn't you find useful / didn't you like doing in class today?*
- *In general, what part of learning the language do you find most difficult?*
- *What do you think you need help with now?*
- *Are there any questions you want to ask me?*

3 Tell the learners that each of them should record themselves at home and send you an email with the link to the recording (the website automatically stores the audio recording online). Let the learners know that the journal will be a private dialogue between you and them, and that you will record an answer and send the link to the audio recording back to them.

4 When you receive an email from a learner, with the link to an audio file, listen to the recording and then record and send a reply, without too much delay. When you record your reply, the focus should be on meaning rather than form, although there's nothing to stop you taking a note of language that each individual learner needs to work on.

53

100 Great Activities: The Best of the Cambridge Handbooks for Language Teachers

5 Persuade the learners to record their journals on a regular basis (once weekly, for instance); doing so should build their confidence in speaking and encourage learner autonomy. Because the learners are able to listen to themselves, too, they will usually try to improve their spoken performance and should become more fluent and accurate over time. Remember that the questions you ask them to answer can be modified to reflect specific activities in class, or specific needs of the learners.

Note

The spoken journal does not always have to be about the learners' language learning. The next time you decide to do this activity for homework, ask the learners to respond to different questions (e.g. about what they did at the weekend, etc.).

Variations

1 If you want to add video, then use the video-record facility available on most smartphones; or a videorecording tool such as Panopto can be used.

2 Apart from using the audio journal for teacher-to-learner communication, you can encourage learner-to-learner interaction. Get the learners to ask each other questions for homework about a topic you (or the learners themselves) decide on, and have the learners respond to each other. If you use this option, ask them to include you when they send the email with the link to their recording. You can also make the recordings public as in Variation 1.

3 For ESP students, you can ask them to do certain tasks specific to the subject / area of interest (e.g. for tourism students can leave a message replying to a customer complaint). If the learners decide on the task themselves, make sure they give you a copy of the task so that you know what the recording is in response to.

Speaking

1.32 Tell me my story

From *Learning One-to-One* by Ingrid Wisniewska

Outline	When teaching one-to-one, your student chooses an interesting anecdote to tell about themself which you then retell back to your student
Author's comment	This activity focuses on the role of the teacher as observer and listener in the one-to-one learning context. The teacher can take a back seat, giving the learner the opportunity to direct the lesson. It is also an opportunity for the teacher to develop their observational skills, identifying areas where the learner has made progress and those that could be explored in future lessons.
Editors' comment	This is an ideal one-to-one activity, but it could be adapted to classroom contexts. For example, having worked on one student's story in front of the class, you then invite other students to tell the story themselves, incorporating your input where possible. The students can work in small groups to reconstruct the story from memory.
Level	Pre-intermediate to Advanced (B1–C1)
Preparation	None

Procedure

1 Invite your student to think of a story or anecdote to tell you. For example:

- *the funniest (or most embarrassing, frightening) thing that ever happened to me*
- *a strange coincidence*
- *a misunderstanding*
- *doing someone a favour.*

2 Listen carefully and when they have finished, tell the story back to your student, using correct English, and introducing helpful and interesting vocabulary and idioms as appropriate.

3 Your student then retells the story using target forms and new vocabulary.

4 Repeat stages 2 and 3 as many times as necessary.

Note
While you are listening, try to picture their experience and the kinds of words and language that will help them express their ideas better.

Acknowledgement
Idea adapted from:
Stevick, E (1989) *Success with Foreign Languages: Seven who Achieved It and What Worked for Them*. Prentice Hall.

100 Great Activities: The Best of the Cambridge Handbooks for Language Teachers

1.33 Three things about me

From *Teaching Large Multilevel Classes* by Natalie Hess

Outline	Students introduce themselves to classmates by mingling and exchanging information about themselves
Editors' comment	This is an excellent ice-breaker, particularly for adolescent or adult classes. You might begin by sharing three interesting facts about yourself, and ask if any members of the class share them, or have something similar. The facts could be past experiences, hobbies, details of your family, ambitions, tastes, even things that annoy you or scare you!
Level	Pre-intermediate to Advanced (B1–C1)
Preparation	None

Procedure

1   Students write down three interesting facts about themselves.

2   Students get up and mingle. They tell one fact about themselves to three different classmates. Each time a fact matches something in the life of the classmate, that classmate acknowledges by saying, for example, *This happened to me too when . . .* , or *I have two big brothers too.*

3   Students continue mingling and try to find as many classmates as they can who have similar 'facts'.

4   Students return to their seats and share any information they have learned with the person sitting next to them.

5   Volunteers speak to the whole class about interesting information they have learned about various classmates.

Speaking

1.34 What are the differences?

From *Keep Talking: Communicative fluency activities for language teaching* by
Friederike Klippel

Outline	In pairs, each student tries to identify differences between his/her own picture and that of the partner, without 'peeping'
Author's comment	This activity uses the information gap principle, which can generate a whole range of motivating speaking activities. It is based on the idea that students hold different bits of information – either slightly different pictures as here or factual information – which must be compared and/or shared in order to do the task.
Editors' comment	Pictures can be either digital or on paper. Either way, you can easily prepare two sets of pictures by taking an original digital line drawing or strip cartoon (make sure it is not copyright) and inserting changes using markers (use a white correction marker to delete lines). Alternatively, take two photos with your phone of the same scene, e.g. a benchtop with a number of objects arranged on it. In the second photo change some of the details, e.g. by substituting or moving objects. But keep a note of the differences as you make them, in case students ask you later what they've missed! It makes it a bit easier if you tell students in advance how many differences there are, so they know when they've finished.
Level	Elementary to Upper Intermediate (A2–B2)
Preparation	Make two versions of the same picture, with minor differences between them (see example photocopiable below). Make enough copies of each version so that half the students have Version A and half have Version B. Example key: 1 left wall noticeboard; 2 bin; 3 flowers; 4 cup on desk; 5 vase on filing cabinet; 6 sun; 7 filing cabinet open drawer; 8 right wall poster; 9 laptop on right hand desk 10 ceiling lights

Procedure

1   Each student works with a partner. One student receives Version A and their partner Version B. By describing their pictures to one another and asking questions they have to determine how many and what differences there are between them. They are not allowed to show their pictures to their partners.

2   When they think they have found all the differences they compare pictures.

Note
If the teacher produces a number of cardboard folders (or big envelopes) with different pictures prepared in this way, students can exchange their pictures with another pair after completion.

Acknowledgement
Idea adapted from:
Byrne, D. and Rixon, S. (1979) *Communication Games*. ELT Guide 1. London: The British Council. Available from: https://www.teachingenglish.org.uk/sites/teacheng/files/pub_F044 ELT-51 ELT Guide-1 - Communication Games_v3.pdf

100 Great Activities: The Best of the Cambridge Handbooks for Language Teachers

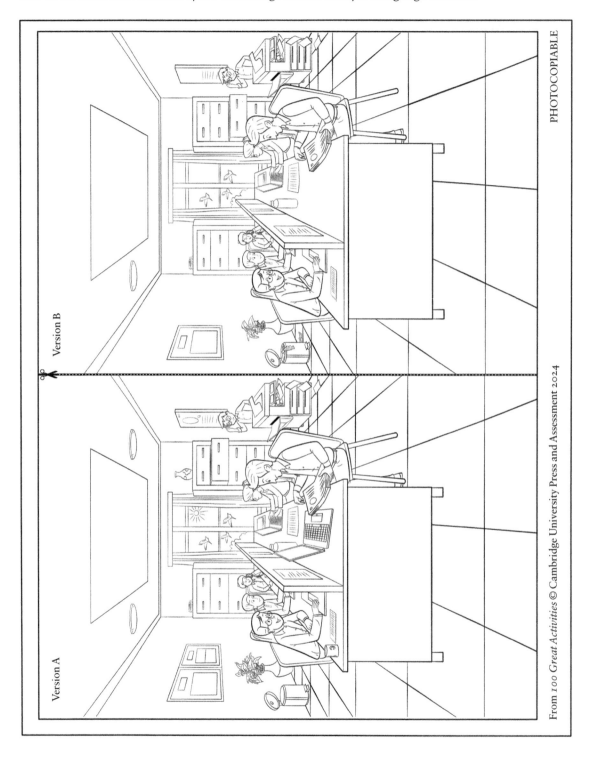

Speaking

1.35 What do we have in common?

From *Learning One-to-One* by Ingrid Wisniewska

Outline	When teaching one-to-one, you and your student exchange personal information
Author's comment	This activity can be used to emphasize the role of the teacher as conversation partner in the one-to-one learning context. Establishing rapport with your student by finding things you have in common is vital to gaining their trust and helping them become more confident in using English. The activity can also help the teacher to identify topics and themes for future lessons.
Editors' comment	This activity can easily be adapted to classroom use: simply model the activity with one student and then put students into pairs to do the same. If you have an odd number of students, form one group of three and draw three – instead of two – intersecting circles. Note also that students don't have to limit themselves to things they like: things in common could be all sorts of things, like daily routines, family or past experiences.
Level	Elementary to Advanced (A2–C1)
Preparation	On a sheet of paper draw two large circles that intersect. Alternatively use a table (see below).

Procedure

1 Explain that the aim of this activity is to make a list of things that you and your student have in common.

2 Tell your student that you are going to ask each other questions and try to fill out the diagram with things that you have in common. For example, in one circle, write the things that you like (but your student does not like), in the other circle write the things that your student likes (but you do not) and in the central overlapping area, write the things that you both like. You could also use this activity to review other grammar areas such as talking about things you can and cannot do, things you have and have not done, things you want to do and do not want to do in the future.

3 Take turns asking each other questions in order to find out how many things you have in common.

4 While talking, model ways of expanding your answers by qualifying them or adding details; and encourage your student to do the same.

5 Keep asking questions until you have ten items in the centre space.

6 When you have reached the target number, summarize your similarities.

7 At this point you may decide to work on some grammar, depending on level, e.g. formation of *yes/no* questions and *wh-* questions or *So do I*, or sentences such as *I like tennis and so do you, I like running, but you don't.*

8 Keep the diagram for future reference when you want to create language practice examples relevant to your student's interests, experiences, etc.

100 Great Activities: The Best of the Cambridge Handbooks for Language Teachers

What do we have in common?

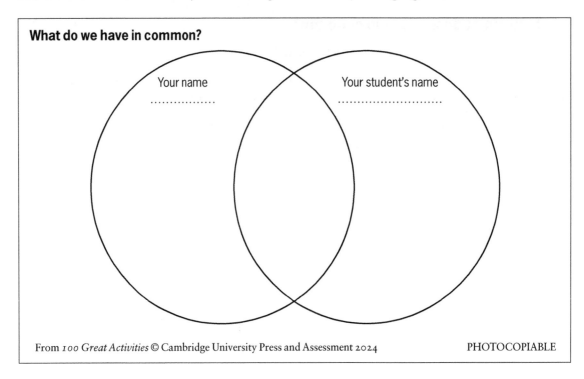

Your name
....

Your student's name
....

From *100 Great Activities* © Cambridge University Press and Assessment 2024   PHOTOCOPIABLE

What do we have in common?

		Your student's name	
		Likes	Dislikes
Your name	Likes		
	Dislikes		

From *100 Great Activities* © Cambridge University Press and Assessment 2024   PHOTOCOPIABLE

Speaking

1.36 Why do you have a monkey in your bag?

From *Five-Minute Activities: A resource book of short activities* by Penny Ur and Andrew Wright

Outline	Students ask each other why they have (imaginary) unexpected things in their bag
Authors' comment	This is a good activity for lighthearted relaxation: after exams, for example, or at the end of term. If the student being asked can't think of a good reason for having a monkey (or whatever) in their bag, allow other students to help by suggesting reasons.
Editors' comment	Such fun – and highly adaptable. For example, it can be used to revise a recently taught lexical set, e.g. fruit and vegetables, clothing, kitchen gadgets or, for learners of specialized English, objects relating to their profession or field of study. Or it could be extended into a role play: At Customs.
Level	Elementary to Upper Intermediate (A2–B2)
Preparation	None

Procedure

1 Empty a bag – yours or one of the students'. Go up to one of the students, give them the bag and ask:

Why do you have a monkey in your bag?

2 The student has to think of a convincing or original reason why there is a monkey in their bag. After giving the reason and answering any questions from the rest of the class, he or she then takes the bag and goes up to another student with the same question, only this time using another object, for example:

Why do you have an axe in your bag?

3 If a student who gets the bag can't think of an object, you might suggest one of the following:

a coffee-cup	a bar of soap
a flower	a carrot
a stone	a doll
a kitten	a bell
a hammer	a trumpet

61

2 Listening

The listening activities in this section invite the learners to respond to something they hear in a variety of ways: by physical action ('Change chairs', 'Obeying instructions'), by suggesting immediate responses or questions ('Predictive listening', 'True or false') or by brief writing or drawing ('Ground-plans', 'Altering and marking'). Significantly, none of them are based on listening 'blind' to the long stretches of audio recordings which often furnish the basis for listening practice in coursebooks and online materials; they rather involve listening and responding to input from the teacher as it is produced or, in one case, sorting out bits of speeches from video clips ('Jumbled statements'). Essentially, all the activities in this section invite learners to listen, understand and respond to spoken texts through engaging with tasks based on interesting and enjoyable challenges.

100 Great Activities: The Best of the Cambridge Handbooks for Language Teachers

2.1 Altering and marking

From *Teaching Listening Comprehension* by Penny Ur

Outline	Students make alterations to pictures, maps, etc. in response to a spoken description
Author's comment	Children particularly very much enjoy tampering with professionally drawn pictures: witness the moustaches, beards and hats drawn on to portraits, and the amount of filling-in, colouring and other kinds of artistic addition made by children to illustrations in their textbooks or storybooks (if allowed!). Note that as you improvise the instructions for this activity, make sure you include a lot of 'redundancy' – pauses or repetition or paraphrases or 'fillers' – in order to give students time to do the drawing or colouring.
Editors' comment	This is a very simple but fun listening task. It could also be turned into a two-way communicative activity, by putting learners into pairs or small groups to give similar instructions to one another.
Level	Beginner to Elementary (A1–A2)
Preparation	Give students a line drawing which has plenty of different people and things in it: see the example below.

Procedure

1 Tell the students to colour bits of the picture according to instructions: for example:

There are flowers on the table. They're red, and they're standing in a black vase. Got that? The vase is black all over, and the flowers are red . . . .

2 Then tell them to take a pencil and add things. For example:

Can you see a little baby in the picture? Ok, I want you to draw a hat on the baby's head. OK? A hat on the baby.

Variation

For beginner learners, this can be used to work on letters. Give them a page full of letters and tell them *The A is blue, the M is red*, and so on. Or: *There's a butterfly sitting on the G, there's a pencil under the F.*

64

100 Great Activities: The Best of the Cambridge Handbooks for Language Teachers

2.2 Change chairs

From *Lessons from Nothing: Activities for language teaching with limited time and resources* by Bruce Marsland

Outline	Students sit in a circle and change chairs in response to your cues
Author's comment	The physical movement required by this activity can be used to add variety in the classroom, and the competitive element is good motivation. Sometimes students will play tactically by trying to describe a specific decoration on somebody's shirt or jacket, for example. This provides a learning opportunity, but it is also important to maintain the natural rhythm of the activity.
Editors' comment	You don't have to limit the commands to clothes: other aspects of personal appearance – provided it's nothing that could lead to embarrassment or distress – could be used (*if you have blue eyes, if you have long hair*). Or anything, really, even if it can't be verified by looking (*if you have a brother, if you came here by bus, if you have a cat*).
Level	Beginner to Intermediate (A1–B1+)
Preparation	None

Procedure

1 Students sit on their chairs in a large circle. Ideally this is done in a large room or outside, but any reasonably uncluttered space will do if there are no obvious physical restrictions to movement, and no dangerous pieces of furniture lying around.

2 The teacher stands in the middle of the circle. There is no chair for the teacher, who then gives the instruction:

Change chairs if you are wearing blue trousers.

3 All students wearing blue trousers then have to stand up and find a new place in the circle which will be a place where another student with blue trousers was sitting. Meanwhile, the teacher sits in one of the vacated places.

4 This leaves a student in the centre of the circle. This student must now do what the teacher has done – make a *Change chairs if . . .* sentence, and then find a vacated chair to sit in. The objective is to get a chair back as soon as possible.

Rationale

This is a good energy-raising exercise for those times when a class has reached its limit for concentration. If you work in a classroom with fixed furniture, taking the students outside and using coats as 'chairs' might give the exercise even more of a sense of fun. Carry on until most of the students have had a turn in the centre, according to the size and enthusiasm of your group.

66

Listening

2.3 Ground-plans

From *Teaching Listening Comprehension* by Penny Ur

Outline	Students label the different areas of a ground-plan according to what they hear
Author's comment	Ground-plans are a kind of map, but consist of regular divisions (as shown below), and could be interpreted as lots of different complexes. In my original version the one shown here was a zoo: but it could equally well be one floor of a shopping mall, the ground floor of a hotel, a supermarket, a garden. Filling in the labels for each area is most easily done using pencil and paper.
Editors' comment	Another very adaptable activity that provides 'live' listening practice. One variation is – once you have reached stage 3 below, and before revealing the ground-plan – to invite individual students to describe it back to you, while you fill in a plan on the board.
Level	Beginner to Elementary (A1–A2)
Preparation	Each student needs a blank copy of the ground-plan shown below, and a list of animals in the zoo. You, as the teacher, have a plan filled in with the names of the animals in each section.

Procedure

1 Distribute the blank ground-plans with the list of animals. Make sure all the students know the meanings of all the names of animals.

2 Tell students you are going to explain where each animal is and they need to write in its name in correct section. They can stop you and ask you questions as you go.

3 Improvise your instructions based on your filled-in ground-plan. Make sure you explain where each animal is at least twice, and leave time for students to write.

4 At the end, display the filled-in plan and let students check if they were right.

Variations

1 Use a basic plan, with square or rectangular blocks, and tell students it is a shopping mall, and describe the locations of the different shops or facilities.

2 Let students take turns telling the class where one of the animals is: everyone fills in each location as it is described.

100 Great Activities: The Best of the Cambridge Handbooks for Language Teachers

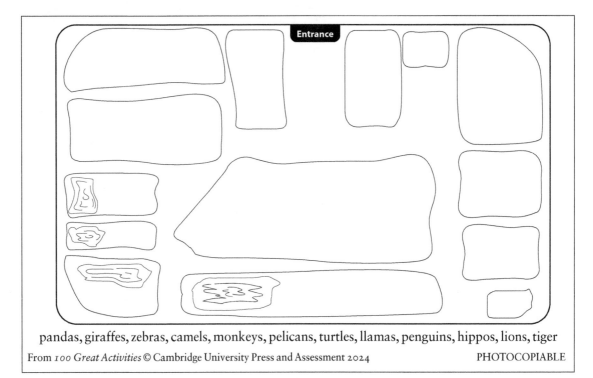

pandas, giraffes, zebras, camels, monkeys, pelicans, turtles, llamas, penguins, hippos, lions, tiger

From *100 Great Activities* © Cambridge University Press and Assessment 2024   PHOTOCOPIABLE

Key

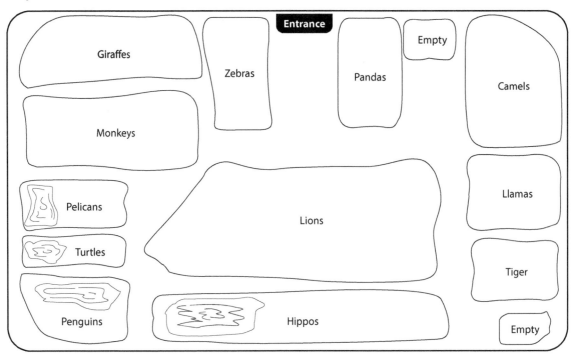

Listening

2.4 Interrupting the story

From *Five-Minute Activities: A resource book of short activities* by Penny Ur and
Andrew Wright

Outline	Students interrupt you with questions as you tell them a story
Authors' comment	With a small class, you don't even need to wait for students to raise their hands, encourage them to call out questions as they think of them. With a bigger class, get them to raise their hands: but the rule is that as soon as someone raises their hand you have to stop and let them ask the question. If you are teaching online, either tell students to use the 'raise hand' icon or to write their questions in the chatbox. In the latter case, as soon as you see a question, you have to answer it.
Editors' comment	This is one of those invaluable activities that integrates listening and speaking, and has the added bonus of being based on storytelling: everyone loves a good story! It also provides some useful practice in asking questions in the past.
Level	Beginner to Intermediate (A1–B1+)
Preparation	Think of a story (a personal anecdote, for example) that you want to tell.

Procedure

1 Tell the students that you are going to begin a story and that they should try to stop you saying more than a few words by asking questions. For example:

You: *The other day . . .*
Student A: *Which day was it?*
You: *It was Tuesday.*
Student B: *Was it in the morning or afternoon?*
You: *Afternoon. Anyway, I was . . .*
Student C: *What time was it?*, etc.

Acknowledgement
We first experienced this technique with Alun Rees in Barcelona.

100 Great Activities: The Best of the Cambridge Handbooks for Language Teachers

2.5 It happened to me

From *Once upon a Time: Using stories in the language classroom* by John Morgan and Mario Rinvolucri

Outline	You recount a personal anecdote and the students respond with stories of their own
Editors' comment	This is deceptively simple but can be hugely productive. Not only does the teacher provide an opportunity for 'live listening', but the students' own stories offer great ways of providing fluency practice and can lead to question-and-answer interactions. You can also ask the class to choose one of the stories and, working in small groups, turn it into a written text which they can then share – thus providing writing and reading practice as well. The teacher can also record the story as he or she tells it, so it is available for further listening, transcription or language analysis.
Level	Elementary to Advanced (A2–C1)
Preparation	Choose an anecdote area such as 'stupid things I've done'. Prepare an anecdote of your own to tell the class.

Possible anecdote ideas

- losing things: documents, passports, handbags, children
- running away: from home, one's job, awkward situations
- near accidents: in the home, on the road
- fear: of things, people, places, imaginary horrors
- positive experiences: a nice surprise, I was lucky, the best present ever
- if only ... stories

Procedure

1 Tell the class your anecdote. (Note: tell it, rather than read it aloud. It will sound more natural and be easier to understand.)

2 Since listening often stimulates memories, by the end of your telling there are likely to be several people in the group who want to tell anecdotes of their own. Get them telling their stories to the whole group.

Listening

2.6 Jumbled statements

From *Using Authentic Video in the Language Classroom* by Jane Sherman

Outline	Students re-order a set of jumbled statements according to the sequence of events from a video
Author's comment	Video drama is the richest source of interactive language and culture apart from real life. Comprehension, of course, is a challenge, involving a mix of utterances, story, background, actions and interactions, accents and context. However, it is a prime ambition of most language students. Comprehension work involves careful choice of texts (by students or teacher) and a range of activities and supports (adopting characters, lead-ins, dossiers, reviews, using subtitles, parallel texts). Jumbled statements engage students in a recap of the action and its meanings. It is suitable for any dramatic sequence, is easy to handle, and needs no preparation.
Editors' comment	Apart from viewing the scene, this activity needs hardly any preparation, but if you want you can prepare the jumbled statements or utterances (Variation 1) in advance. For the utterances, you may want to prepare with subtitles or transcripts if available – but remember that these may be inaccurate, so check.
Level	Pre-intermediate to Upper Intermediate (B1–B2)
Preparation	A short video, or extract from a dramatic movie, with a clear sequence of events.

Procedure

1 While viewing, write up a set of statements in jumbled order about the action on the board. Alternatively, students write one event each while they view; then put them all on the board in jumbled order, e.g.:

The priest pulled the girl away.
A man fell off the roof.
The pigeon flew up to the roof.
The boss sent the man away.
Charlie counted the money.
(From *On the Waterfront*)

2 Students discuss and expand each statement (*Who? When? Why?*), then try to sequence them correctly.

3 View again for students to get more detail and check the sequencing.

Variations

1 Use utterances instead of events. While viewing, each student writes down one thing that someone says (or the teacher can write down several). After viewing, students/teacher write up all the utterances on the board, then decide who said them, to whom, what about, when, where, why and in what manner. Students arrange them in chronological order and review to check their impressions.

2 Students can create a quiz for others by selecting a number of utterances and recording the correct answers (who, when, etc.) separately.

71

100 Great Activities: The Best of the Cambridge Handbooks for Language Teachers

2.7 Obeying instructions

From *Teaching Listening Comprehension* by Penny Ur

Outline	Students obey commands that you give them
Author's comment	It's very tempting to take a traditional game and transfer it to the classroom as it is: but like many other games, it may need tweaking a bit to make it work as a language learning activity. So, for example, in the traditional version of 'Simon says' anyone who makes a mistake is 'out'; but that means that they stop playing, and we really want our students to participate as much as possible: hence the version suggested below.
Editors' comment	This is a game that was turned into a methodology called Total Physical Response (TPR) but in fact dates back much further than that. Proponents of the Direct Method encouraged learners to perform sentences they had heard in order to demonstrate their understanding and to reinforce the sentence patterns in memory. More recently, research has shown that children retain the meanings of new words and expressions in their own language better when they have enacted them. It follows that the same effects would occur in a second language – and not just for children.
Level	Beginner to Elementary (A1–A2)
Preparation	None

Procedure

1   At the elementary level, commands may be as simple as: stand up, sit down, go to (something), put your hand on (something), take the (something), look at the (something), open (something) ...

2   Then move on to 'Simon says': only the command prefixed by the words 'Simon says' is to be obeyed, the rest ignored. When a student makes a mistake, he or she is not 'out' but continues playing. At the end of the game, ask who made four mistakes or more? who made three? two? one? none? Congratulate those who made fewer than three!

Variations

1   Instead of 'Simon says', use 'Please' as the indicator that the students have to do the action; or 'Don't' to indicate that they should not.

2   The teacher gives a simple command to do a physical action, but simultaneously performs an action themself which may or may not be the same as the command. So students have to be on the alert, and perform the command they hear, not necessarily what they see the teacher do. This adds motivation and makes students concentrate on listening.

3   Other kinds of command can ask students to respond not with actions but with miming moods (*You are afraid! You are sad! You are angry*), or animals (*You are a cat! You are a butterfly!*) or physical attributes or sensations (*You are tall! You are strong! You are cold!*).

72

Listening

2.8 Oral retelling by students

From *Using Folktales* by Eric K. Taylor

Outline	Students retell a story that you tell them
Author's comment	Especially with mixed levels, some students can listen to a story, even with a lot of miming, sketches, and explanation by the teacher, and still miss key parts (or the whole point!). By having students tell the story back to you, you provide one more review for the students who didn't quite get it, while at the same time providing an opportunity to use the new language encountered in the story. It also gives you an opportunity to find out what students understood.
Editors' comment	You might help students tell the story by starting it off yourself, and by writing key words and phrases on the board even before they start. Another possibility, if the class is monolingual and you speak their language, is to invite students to recall and relate the story in their L1 first, before getting them to tell it in English.
Level	Beginner to Intermediate (A1–B1+)
Preparation	Tell a story to the students, or have them read and study a story on their own.

Procedure

1 Tell students that you want them to tell the story back to you. (The first time you do this, especially with lower levels, it may take some prompting before they figure out what you want.)

2 As students tell the story back to you, write key words and phrases on the board; this helps students associate oral and written forms and helps more visual learners.

3 Ask questions so that all students are included.

4 Drawing simple sketches during the telling helps associate words with meanings for lower-level students who may still be missing some of what they are listening to.

Variation
Group students' statements by episode; this begins to draw students' attention to the underlying structure.

100 Great Activities: The Best of the Cambridge Handbooks for Language Teachers

2.9 Predictive listening

From *Using Newspapers in the Classroom* by Paul Sanderson

Outline	Students are challenged to predict the next word as you pause when reading aloud a text
Author's comment	An important aim of this activity is not for your students to always get the 'right' answer, but for them to follow the story and suggest plausible answers.
Editors' comment	This procedure replicates a real-life strategy that we use when listening to (or reading) input: we are often able to predict, if not the exact word that is coming, then at least the kind of word or kind of phrase. Prediction is a useful strategy to encourage, and the activity can be fun. But its success does depend on the students understanding the main content of the text and knowing most of the vocabulary: hence the careful preparation as recommended by the author. It can be used with any text, not just newspaper articles; and can practise reading prediction as well as listening, by using a written text projected on the board.
Level	Intermediate to Advanced (B1+–C1)
Preparation	Select a newspaper story which you think will interest your students. Go through the article carefully to find places in the text where you could stop before a particular word, and your students could try to guess what this word might be. When selecting which words (i.e. answers) that you want your students to guess, there are two possible types of answer you can choose: you can stop before obvious 'right/wrong' or limited-possibility answers, e.g. the final word of collocations, fixed expressions or grammatical constructions. Alternatively, you can stop before answers where a number of more creative, open answers would be possible. This requires your students to use their imaginations; their offering plausible answers here shows that they are following the sequence of the story as it unfolds.

Procedure

1 Write the headline of the article you have chosen on the board and check that your students understand it. Then tell your students a brief summary of the article and, as you do so, pre-teach any key vocabulary in the text, but none that is contained in the answers you want your students to guess.

2 Explain to your students that you are going to read the newspaper article aloud to them, but that you will stop in several places before the next word. When you stop, they should call out what they think the next word will be in the context of the story.

3 Begin reading the article aloud up to the first point where your students have to suggest the next word, stop, and make a clear gesture to your students that they should begin calling out their ideas.

4 Let your students continue doing so until they have exhausted all their ideas, then tell them the correct solution.

5 If your students are giving you answers which are clearly going in the wrong direction, this is an indication that they have misunderstood something or have been unable to follow. In this case, reread the previous section, explaining it if necessary.

Listening

6 Continue this procedure for the rest of the article.

7 Point out to your students that during reading, we are subconsciously predicting and anticipating language, based on our knowledge of language as well as our understanding of the text. This can help us in our reading, for we are often reading to confirm our expectations.

Acknowledgement
My thanks to Silvia Stephan, who suggested this activity.

100 Great Activities: The Best of the Cambridge Handbooks for Language Teachers

2.10 Talk like a robot

From *Activities for Very Young Learners* by Herbert Puchta and Karen Elliott

Outline	Students listen to instructions and carry them out, pretending to be robots
Authors' comment	Total Physical Response (TPR) activities help children understand instructions in a stress-free and fast way. The relationship between language and the body seems to play an important role in that process. Once learners are at ease with the new language, give a few 'surprise instructions' – combinations of the new input and previously learnt language, e.g. Sing like a robot. Walk like a duck. Later, encourage children to come up with suggestions of their own.
Editors' comment	This can be a lot of fun – and could be tried out on older learners too, although maybe substituting well-known public figures (e.g. actors) for *robot*.
Level	Beginner to Intermediate (A1–B2)
Preparation	None

Procedure

1 In a computer-like, flat voice say, *We're all robots now. Hello, robots! It's good to see you.*

2 Carry on talking in this way, encouraging the children to copy you. Then point to the children in front of you and say (still in your 'robot' voice) *Robots, can you say something?* Give the children a bit of time and wait for them to make an attempt at talking like a robot. When a child has said something, praise them, and repeat what they have said, modelling the robot voice. Get the whole class to repeat it.

3 Give instructions, and do robot-like actions or mimes for the children to copy, for example:

Walk like a robot.
Dance like a robot.
Write on the board like a robot.
Make a phone call like a robot.
Play football like a robot.
Drive a car like a robot.
Drink a glass of juice like a robot.
Eat an ice cream like a robot.

Variations

1 For older children, add 'slowly' or 'fast' to the instructions to make the game more challenging (e.g. *Walk slowly like a robot. Eat an ice cream quickly like a robot.*).

2 Play robot 'Simon says': the children only follow your instructions if you include *robot* (e.g. *Jump like a robot*). If you say, for example, *Point to the window,* the children who do the action (by mistake) need to sit down on the floor and miss a turn.

3 Use the question form *Can you . . . ?* instead of direct instructions, e.g. *Can you play football like a robot? Can you say 'hello' like a robot?*

76

Listening

2.11 The teacher's autobiography

From *Dictation: New methods, new possibilities* by Paul Davis and Mario Rinvolucri

Outline	Dictate sentences about yourself, and students decide which are true and which are false
Authors' comment	The example we give below was used with a lower-intermediate group on only the fifth meeting with them. None of the students had sufficient information to pick out the false statements from prior knowledge. They simply had to work on feel, intuition and, in some cases, internal evidence within the sets of statements.
Editors' comment	Scott does a reduced version of this with only six to nine sentences, some of which are true, some false. The students copy down all the sentences and then decide between them which are true and which are false. But it's a nice idea to get them, as individuals, to write down only the ones they think are false. It's also a great technique for embedding a target language feature, such as time adverbials (two years ago . . .) or verb phrases (I like doing . . .) which you can then highlight after the guesswork has been done.
Level	Any
Preparation	Write several batches of four statements about periods in your life. In each batch of four, three should be true and one should be false. For example:

> *I went to primary school.*
> *I didn't want to learn to read.*
> *I began to love reading.*
> *I loved reading history books.*

(You can make the language of the statements easier or more difficult to fit the level of your class.)

Procedure

1 Tell the students they are going to hear sets of four statements. One of the statements in each set will be false. They are to write down only the statement they believe to be false.

2 Read each group of statements three times. Suggest that the students listen carefully for the first two times and only write during or after the third reading. Give a fourth reading if you are asked to.

3 After the selective dictation get the students working in small groups, comparing the sentences they picked out as false. Give them copies of the sets of statements and time to read them through.

4 Finally, read out the false statements.

Variation

A natural follow-up to the teacher autobiographical dictation is to ask students to prepare similar sets of statements which they then read/dictate to each other. In this way students explore one another's pasts.

Acknowledgement

This exercise type was suggested by Gail Morare who worked with the Adult Migrant Education Service in Melbourne, Australia.

100 Great Activities: The Best of the Cambridge Handbooks for Language Teachers

2.12 True or false

From *Pictures for Language Learning* by Andrew Wright

Outline	Students respond to true or false statements relating to a picture
Author's comment	This true/false game can be used when the teacher wants the students simply to repeat what he or she says. The teacher can hold up a picture and make a statement which is true or false. If the statement is true, the students repeat what the teacher says. If it is false, they remain silent or correct it. In this way the students have the advantage of repetition practice with its emphasis on pronunciation, but at the same time must think about the meaning of what they are saying. The teacher can add humour to the activity by pretending to be tired or shortsighted. This 'explains' why the teacher is making so many mistakes.
Editors' comment	This basic idea is multi-skill: it starts out as listening comprehension, and develops into speaking, reading and writing. If you are teaching through an online video-conferencing platform like Zoom, then it's easy to display the pictures through screensharing, and then elicit responses either orally or through the chatbox.
Level	Beginner to Elementary (A1–A2)
Preparation	Prepare clear pictures either on paper or projected on the board.

Procedure

1 The teacher displays a picture.

2 The teacher makes a statement about the picture which is either true or false. If it is false, the students either stay silent or correct the teacher. For example:

Teacher: (*showing a picture of a woman playing tennis*) She's playing football.
Students: (*stay silent*)
OR
Students: No, she isn't. She's playing tennis.

Variations

1 The students are given a lot of sentences about a picture, some of which are true and some of which are false. They copy out all those which apply to a picture they are shown.

2 The students are given a text describing a picture, which contains false statements. The students rewrite the text accurately.

3 The students are given different texts describing a picture correctly. They rewrite their text introducing untrue elements. The students then exchange texts and try to find the untrue elements in each other's work.

4 Students working in pairs write true and/or false sentences describing a picture. The pairs of students exchange sentences and decide which sentences written by the other pair are true and which are false.

3 Reading

Typically, coursebooks expect learners to respond to written texts by answering a series of comprehension questions. Depending on how these questions are framed, they may not in fact test comprehension at all, but instead test common sense, general knowledge or simply word recognition. All of the activities in this section, however, invite learners to respond to written texts in more interesting and original ways – such as marking up the text with symbols ('Using symbols'), collecting and comparing 'found' texts ('An A–Z of signs in English'), performing instructions ('Classroom language'), reducing the text ('Vanishing stories'), task planning ('Celebrity dinner party'), or completing a 'damaged' text ('Strip cloze').

100 Great Activities: The Best of the Cambridge Handbooks for Language Teachers

3.1 An A–Z of signs in English

From *Intercultural Language Activities* by John Corbett

Outline	Students collect and discuss examples of English used in street signs and advertising in their own community
Author's comment	'An A–Z of signs in English' invites learners to observe and reflect on the global English that is becoming part of the linguistic landscape of many countries, and to share their observations and reflections with partners. The activity encourages learners to think critically about the appropriation of English as a second language around the world.
Editors' comment	This is a great way of raising – and sharing – awareness about multilingualism in general, and about the pervasive presence of English in particular. Given that most, if not all, learners will have phones, this activity is very easy to set up and, as the author notes, can be adapted to English-speaking environments. We've categorized it as a reading activity because it alerts learners to the reading opportunities that exist in the 'real world'.
Level	Elementary to Advanced (A2–C1) and above
Preparation	This activity will need to be spread over two lessons and involves learners looking for English signs in the community in their own time.

Procedure

1   Divide the class into groups and tell each group that its members are required to go into their community after school, and photograph (or note down) examples of signs (including road signs, publicity, public notices, hoardings, etc.) in English and/or other languages used in the area.

2   Explain that each group should collect signs that represent as much of the alphabet, A–Z, as possible. They can be flexible about which word in the sign represents a letter in the alphabet. You can project some examples you have collected yourself.

3   In a following lesson, the learners share their signs and see how many letters of the alphabet they have covered. Then they re-classify them according to their content, e.g. advertisements for food, drink, clothes, public notices, etc. They should then produce a poster arranging the signs on it according to their content, which they can share with the other groups and discuss their findings, e.g. were most of the signs in English for food?

4   More advanced learners can then discuss some of the following questions:
- *What kinds of product are advertised in English?*
- *Do any signs use a mixture of languages?*
- *What reasons can you think of for using English on signs in a non-English-speaking country?*
- *Is the use of English on signs something you should be angry about, or afraid of – or is it a development that you welcome?*

5   If learners are participating in an online intercultural exchange, they can go online and share their experience of signs in English with their online partners. Is English used similarly in signs in different places? Are similar things advertised in English in different places?

80

Reading

Example signs in English

A sign about cellphone use in Beijing

A sign in a park in Mexico city

A warning sign in Singapore

A subway sign in Paris

From *100 Great Activities* © Cambridge University Press and Assessment 2024   PHOTOCOPIABLE

Variation for learners in an English-speaking environment
This activity can be adapted for other languages – for example, is there evidence of signs in Arabic, Chinese, French, German, Spanish, Polish or Punjabi in public spaces in this country? Particularly fruitful areas for exploration are restaurants and department stores.

100 Great Activities: The Best of the Cambridge Handbooks for Language Teachers

3.2 Celebrity dinner party

From *The Internet and the Language Classroom: A practical guide for teachers 2nd edition* by Gavin Dudeney

Outline	Students find out about celebrities and plan seating for a dinner party where they are guests
Author's comment	This activity is a classic, and pre-dates the common use of technologies in teaching. There is a lot going on in the process – speaking, reading and writing – and the activity involves negotiating skills, justifying arguments, agreeing and disagreeing, and more. Technology gives learners access to world knowledge they may not possess, and can play a part in the visuals and follow-up activities – a good example of technology enhancing, rather than replacing, a productive activity. This can also be adapted for business English classes, using appropriate figures from the world of business, finance, etc.
Editors' comment	You can introduce any further limitations or definitions you like for the guests. For example, you might say that the four people have to be from a certain area (entertainment or politics, for example); or they have to be people who are no longer alive (they are brought back to life for the purposes of this dinner party!); or that they have to include two men and two women. You can also raise the number: they might want to invite five or six.
Level	Intermediate to Advanced (B1+–C1)
Preparation	Plan your own celebrity dinner party as a model to introduce the activity – choose four people (living or dead) who you would like to have at your dinner party and reasons why you have chosen them. Brainstorm a couple of questions you would like to ask each of them at your party. Add the photos to a traditional table seating plan – using PowerPoint, or similar – and work out how you would seat your guests for maximum potential.

Procedure

1 Introduce the activity by showing your celebrity dinner table. Tell your learners that they are going to plan a party and that they can invite anyone they want to invite – living or dead. Tell them about your guests: who they are; why you have invited them, why they are sitting where they are sitting, and what you would like to ask them.

2 Divide the class into pairs and ask them to discuss the four people they would like to invite to their party – they must agree on four between them, in each pair. Alternatively, provide a list of famous people, living or dead, from which they have to choose four. The less famous they are, the better, as this will encourage more research.

3 Learners may not know much about the people they have chosen, so the next part of the activity gives them a chance to find out some more, while practising their search skills.

82

Reading

4   Give your learners 15 minutes to research online the people they are interested in inviting. Remind them that they will need to give reasons why they have invited them, explain where everyone will be sitting, and examples of the questions they would ask each guest.

5   Put pairs together to discuss their arrangements. They should explain:
  • who they have invited and why;
  • why they have certain people sitting next to each other;
  • where they themselves would sit;
  • what they would like to ask their guests.

Variations
There are plenty of opportunities to adapt and extend this activity. Students might like to plan the menu for the evening (are any of the celebrity guests vegetarian?), or perhaps arrange an interview with their favourite guest. The interview can then be written up, recorded or even filmed using a smartphone.

100 Great Activities: The Best of the Cambridge Handbooks for Language Teachers

3.3 Classroom language

From *Working with Words: A guide to teaching and learning vocabulary* by Ruth Gairns and Stuart Redman

Outline	Students practise using useful words and phrases used in the coursebook or classroom interaction
Authors' comment	This is an activity for low-level students to learn and practise vocabulary commonly used by teachers in classroom instructions, and in rubrics in published materials. The main focus is vocabulary acquisition, but the presentation text tests reading skills with an engaging puzzle element, and the practice provides a good deal of student interaction. Constant exposure alone usually guarantees that these items will eventually be absorbed, but one can hasten the process in a positive way by designing classroom activities that will incorporate many of these items and so avoid confusion or misunderstanding at a later date. The activity is very easy to set up in the classroom, but learners could also use it on their own for self-study. It is deceptively simple.
Editors' comment	A very helpful exercise to do in the classroom with learners who are having problems coping with coursebook instructions, but quite tricky and time-consuming to design on one's own, so this is a really useful contribution. A follow-up might be to ask students to scan through their coursebooks and look for one or more examples of the vocabulary they have used there.
Level	Beginner to Elementary (A1–A2)
Preparation	You will need to prepare the text below for display on the board, and make copies of (or send to students' digital devices) the worksheet.

Note

There are some vocabulary items which frequently appear in language activity instructions. Common among these are:

true/false	instruction/description/suggestion/opinion
tick/cross	get into pairs / groups
regular/irregular	grid/chart/map/form
gaps/blanks	fill in / cross out / leave out / underline
offer/accept/refuse/invite	top/middle/bottom

Procedure

1 Ask the students to study Part 1 of the Worksheet.

2 The following items could then be elicited and written on the board.

to put a tick/cross	*to fill in something, e.g. to fill in a blank*
to leave out something	*top/bottom*
to underline something	*true/false*
to cross out something	*a map/chart*

3 Then invite students to do Part 2 of the Worksheet.

84

Reading

Worksheet
Part 1

time	6:30
place	Rome
reason	tourism

✓ There is a tick at the beginning of this sentence.
In this sentence the word cat is underlined.
There are two blanks in the next sentence.
My _____ lives _____ Venezuela.
In the next sentence the blanks are filled in.
My brother lives in Venezuela.
The fifth word in ~~this~~ sentence is crossed out.
2 + 2 = 4 is true. 2 + 2 = 5 is false.
At the side of Part 1 of this worksheet there is a map of Italy.
At the top of this piece of paper there is a table.
I am going to leave out one word in the next sentence.
I come to _____ by bus.
I left out the word 'school' in the sentence above.

Part 2

1 Write your name above this sentence and underline it.
2 Cross out the third word in the first sentence.
3 Draw a map of your country in the box on the right.
4 Put a tick at the end of this question.
5 Leave out question 6.
6 Ask your teacher a question.
7 Write a false sentence about yourself at the bottom of the worksheet.
8 Put a cross in the middle of your map.
9 Fill in the blanks in question 10.
10 My name is _____ _____.
11 Is the answer to question 10 true or false?
12 Get into groups and check your answers.

From *100 Great Activities* © Cambridge University Press and Assessment 2024   PHOTOCOPIABLE

100 Great Activities: The Best of the Cambridge Handbooks for Language Teachers

3.4 Strip cloze

From *Using Newspapers in the Classroom* by Paul Sanderson

Outline	Students reconstruct missing letters, words or phrases blacked out in a newspaper article
Editors' comment	The original was planned using an overhead projector and laying a strip of paper over part of the text (hence the activity name); but today we can use digital tools, as suggested below. The arbitrary 'black-out' shape means that sometimes only letters are missing, sometimes words, sometimes full phrases. Of course, this procedure can be applied to any reading text, not just newspaper articles.
Level	Elementary to Advanced (A2–C1)
Preparation	Select an article you think will interest your students and project it on the board.

Procedure

1 Show your students the article and allow them enough time to read it through from beginning to end. Deal with any vocabulary or language problems at this stage of the activity. If you wish, you can discuss the content and/or the theme of the article with your students.

2 Now insert a narrow rectangular shape (if you have copied the text into a Word document, you can use, for example, the 'Insert' → 'Shapes' tool) to overlay a part of the article – either vertically or at an angle (see example below).

3 Begin reading the article aloud, but stop before the first word (partly) concealed by the strip.

4 Ask your students to call out the word, spelling it if you think this is necessary.

5 Check their answer by continuing reading to the end of the line and then contracting the strip to reveal the correct solution.

6 Continue this procedure for the rest of the article.

7 When you have worked through the whole article, place the strip on the article in a new position, pair students and ask them to work through the article together.

Variation

Repeat the procedure at the end of your first reading by moving the strip to another position.

86

Reading

Acknowledgement
Text from:
Barker, W.H. and Sinclair, C. (1917) 'How Wisdom Became The Property of the Human Race', *West African Folk-Tales*. George G. Harrap and Company, London.

100 Great Activities: The Best of the Cambridge Handbooks for Language Teachers

3.5 Using symbols

From *Teaching and Developing Reading Skills* by Peter Watkins

Outline	Students use symbols to record their responses to a text
Author's comment	I chose this because of the very positive feedback from teachers that I have shared it with – many of whom use it again and again. The activity promotes affective engagement with texts (whereas many reading activities are solely a cognitive challenge) and the sharing of real emotions/reactions builds community. It is very easy to set up and can be used in conjunction with other reading tasks (e.g. answering questions). It can be used in EFL classes and many ESP/EAP contexts. Learners can also add symbols to the list (e.g. one of my students invented a symbol for 'this makes me angry').
Editors' comment	This is a great way in to any text, and addresses the problem that so many classroom texts are dealt with at the level of comprehension and/or language analysis, but ignore the learner's own response to the text. At higher levels, we can envisage using it with literary texts as well.
Level	Elementary to Advanced (A2–C1)
Preparation	Plan a series of symbols that learners could use to express their reactions to the text, e.g.:

✓	=	I agree with this.
✗	=	I disagree with this.
?	=	I don't understand fully.
Λ	=	I need/want more explanation.
↔	=	Compare this to …
!	=	This is surprising / shocking.
lol	=	This is funny.

Procedure

1   Explain the symbols to the learners.

2   If possible, display the symbols on the classroom wall, so that learners can refer to them whenever they are needed and in future lessons if the activity is repeated.

3   Lead in to the text in the usual way.

4   Ask the learners to annotate the text using the symbols.

5   Learners compare and explain their responses in small groups.

6   Develop a whole class discussion, comparing how learners responded.

Reading

Note

The activity works well with texts that are likely to elicit a range of opinions and attitudes. Where learners use the Λ symbol, they can be encouraged to follow this up and find the information from alternative sources. Reading online makes this particularly easy to do.

The Λ and ? symbols allow readers to consider inadequacies in the writing as the cause of communication breakdown, rather than always assuming that their own language resources are the cause of any difficulties in communication. The ↔ symbol allows learners to explicitly make links to existing knowledge or alternative views. This is a key part of the comprehension process.

100 Great Activities: The Best of the Cambridge Handbooks for Language Teachers

3.6 Vanishing stories

From *Once upon a Time: Using stories in the language classroom* by John Morgan and
Mario Rinvolucri

Outline	Students reduce a text without loss of grammaticality or sense
Authors' comment	This is an excellent exercise to do with tired students, as it requires and gets high concentration. Perhaps this is because so many skills and operations are happening almost at once: • silent reading for meaning • reading aloud: intonation; rhythm • checking inflectional possibilities; checking syntactic possibilities; listening very closely for meaning.
Editors' comment	This activity really concentrates attention on language at several levels – lexical, morphological and syntactical. At the same time it exploits the tension between the rules of grammar, on the one hand, and creativity on the other. The activity is called 'Vanishing stories', but the text needn't be a narrative. Scott has used very short poems quite successfully, as in the example below.
Level	Intermediate (B1) and above
Preparation	Find or write a short text of about 30–40 words, preferably one that comprises a single sentence. For example: *There was an Old Man with a beard,* *Who said, 'It is just as I feared!* *Two Owls and a Hen,* *Four Larks and a Wren,* *Have all built their nests in my beard!'* (Edward Lear)

Procedure

1 Write the text on the board.

2 Explain to the students that they are going to reduce this text as much as they can. Give them these rules:
   • You may take out one word.
   • You may take out two consecutive words.
   • You may take out three consecutive words.
   • You must not add anything.
   • You must not change or modify any words.
   • You must not move any words.
   • You may delete, change or delete punctuation as needed.
   • After each deletion the student who has proposed it must read the remaining text aloud: this must be grammatically correct and must have a meaning, though the meaning may change as the exercise progresses.

90

Reading

3   As soon as a student suggests a deletion, rub it out at once, without hesitation. If the resultant sentence is wrong and the student does not realise it, turn silently to the others and ask their opinion with your face. If no one realises it is wrong, put back the word(s) deleted without comment. Here's how it might work using the above text:

There was an Old Man with a beard,
Who said, 'It is just as I feared!
~~Two Owls and~~ a Hen,
Four Larks and a Wren,
Have all built their nests in my beard!'

There was an Old Man ~~with a beard,~~
Who said, 'It is just as I feared!
a Hen,
Four Larks and a Wren,
Have all built their nests in my beard!'

There was an Old Man
Who said, 'It is just as I feared!
a Hen,
Four Larks and a Wren,
~~Have all~~ built their nests in my beard!'

. . . and so on. The group may well be able to reduce the original sentence to one word (though this should not be an absolute aim).

Note

In this exercise there is no need for you to speak at all. You can demand re-readings or indicate doubt by gesture. This makes the students concentrate much harder on the board and leaves space for them to think. Give time for the student you are working with at any given moment to decide for themself whether the latest deletion leaves the sentence acceptable or not.

Acknowledgement

We learnt this exercise from our exposure to Silent Way, though we do not know whether this form of reduction was invented by Caleb Gattegno, thought up by people round him or indeed incorporated in Silent Way practice from earlier thinking by others.

4 Writing

Writing is a composite skill involving the ability to integrate different levels of knowledge, from the lower-level skills, such as spelling, punctuation and sentence construction, to the more comprehensive ones, such as text organization, coherence, and the way different written genres are structured. The activities in this section target these areas, either in isolation ('Bingo', 'Making mine long', 'Creative copying') or in combination ('Running dictation', 'Dictogloss' or 'Delayed reverse translations'). What distinguishes these activities is that the emphasis is typically on collaboration ('Collective story writing'), interaction ('Foodies', 'Paper talk') and/or creativity ('Acrostic' and 'Once upon a time', among many others). Hence, they provide a marked contrast to the somewhat solitary and formulaic nature of traditional classroom writing activities such as writing letters or essays.

100 Great Activities: The Best of the Cambridge Handbooks for Language Teachers

4.1 Acrostic

From *Writing Simple Poems: Pattern poetry for language acquisition* by Vicki L. Holmes and Margaret R. Moulton

Outline	Students write simple acrostic poems
Authors' comment	The acrostic can be a simple poem to write, but it can be made more challenging. Spelling is emphasized for the key word of the acrostic, but use of the dictionary can also be taught to enrich vocabulary.
Editors' comment	Writing acrostic poems is so easy and enjoyable, I don't know why teachers don't do it more! Penny uses it with students' names, asking them to write an acrostic for their own name, and then perhaps for the name of a classmate (with the condition that it has to be nice, avoid anything that might hurt the feelings of the classmate!). Or use any other concept, like those suggested by the authors, but preferably one that the students have some kind of personal feelings about.
Level	Elementary to Intermediate (A2–B1+)
Preparation	None

Procedure

1   Explain what an acrostic is: that it spells out a word in a column and then explains the word in words or phrases beginning with each letter of the word. Show the students one of the samples below (choose one appropriate for the level) and ask them to identify the word (FRIEND).

Funny	Furry face	Few people are
Real	Red hair	Real friends
Interesting	Intelligent eyes	In my life. I
Enjoyable	Ears that hear everything	Enjoy seeing true, not
Nice	Nose that sniffs	New friends every
Delightful	Dog of my dreams	Day

2   Select a word or name that is an example of the acrostic students will be writing: your name, a place-name, a character's name, a book title, an animal, a science or maths concept, or any noun about which the students have knowledge. For a short poem, for instance, you might select the word 'school', whereas for a longer example you might select the proper name of your school. Using capital letters, write the word on the board in a column:

S
C
H
O
O
L

3   Explain to the students that you are going to write a poem made up of words (or phrases or sentences, depending on the level of students) that begin with these letters and that express your knowledge and attitude toward it. If, for instance, you selected the word 'school' you might then say: I know that 'students' and 'studying' are part of school. I think I like 'students' better, so I'll use that.

94

Writing

Using the 'S' in the column that spells school, write the word student:

Student

Make sure the first letter is larger and bolder than the rest so that it is obvious you are spelling the word in the left column.

4   Continue with the next letter of the word, asking students for suggestions of words. Continue until all the letters have a word, phrase or sentence attached. Here are examples of two possible poems:

Student	Students learn from teachers
Community	Cool stuff that will
Helpfully	Help them earn credits in
Offering	Order to go to college and have
Opportunities	Opportunities to better their
Learning	Lives

5   Your students should now be ready to practise writing their own acrostics individually, in pairs, or in small groups. This is a good opportunity to encourage them to browse through dictionaries or the glossaries of their coursebooks for words that start with a particular letter.

Uses
- to introduce each student and their name
- to explore attitudes and emotions towards an idea
- to define or describe an animal, a geographic location, an abstract concept, or some other content-related idea
- to explain a concept in the student's native language that may defy direct translation but could be described
- to summarize the plot or describe a character in a book the student has read

100 Great Activities: The Best of the Cambridge Handbooks for Language Teachers

4.2 Bingo

From *Teaching English Spelling: A practical guide* by Ruth Shemesh and Sheila Waller

Outline	Students play bingo with words using particular spelling patterns
Authors' comment	Bingo is a seriously fun exercise that easily adapts itself to spelling. Teachers benefit from the game's ease of preparation and its flexibility, which allows for adjustments in the number of squares as well as choice of content. Students benefit from a highly motivating reinforcement activity in which anyone can be a winner. Simultaneously, students use various language skills (reading, writing, listening, speaking) to complete the task.
Editors' comment	This can be used to practise any set of vocabulary items, not just spelling. You don't necessarily need a 'card' divided into sections, just tell students to write down any six (or up to ten) items from those on the board. Then call out the words in random order and students cross off the ones they hear. Perhaps have two winners – the first to cross off all items and the last: that way you get through all the items, and keep the challenge going until the end. Another variation, with a monolingual class, is to call out the L1 equivalent instead of the actual English word.
Level	Beginner to Elementary (A1–A2)
Preparation	None

Procedure

1   The class brainstorms at least 20 words, some of which follow one spelling pattern, e.g. 'a–e', and some of which follow another, e.g. 'ay'. Write students' suggestions on the board. Also, on the board draw the following Bingo card for them to copy into their notebooks.

Bingo!		

2   Students choose words from the board to fill up their cards.

3   Call out the words in random order. If the students hear a word that is on their card, they cross it out.

4   As the teacher, you can decide on the method of winning: either the first to complete one row, one column, one diagonal or the whole card. The winner calls out 'Bingo' and has to read out the words that form the winning card.

Variation

In order to increase class participation, you might like to have the students take turns calling out words from the board which are NOT on their card.

96

Writing

4.3 Bouncing dialogue

From *Games for Language Learning 3rd edition* by Andrew Wright, David Betteridge and Michael Buckby

Outline	Students interact with one another through a written dialogue
Authors' comment	You can add to the amount of work done by asking each pair to bounce two different dialogues between each other at the same time.
Editors' comment	This activity can be done either on paper or through a messaging tool like WhatsApp. Other possibilities for the initial instructions: each of the partners sends a question to the other; they reply and add a follow-up question. Or: each sends an optimistic (or pessimistic) forecast for the future, the partner responds with *Yes, but . . .* and adds an objection. Each partner continues the correspondence with *Yes, but . . . .* An alternative: *Yes, and . . .* , adding an additional point in support of what their partner said. After a few minutes learners are invited to read out their chat to the class.
Level	Elementary to Advanced (A2–C1)
Preparation	If you are doing this online, make sure students have the relevant communication tools ready on their smartphones (or other digital devices).

Procedure

1   Ask learners to work in pairs to create a dialogue between two characters. For example, one learner can be a parent, the other a teenage child, and the situation is that the teenager was given permission to come home at midnight, but came home at two o'clock in the morning.

2   Tell the learners that they must not speak, but only read silently and write in response as they bounce the dialogue to and fro between them.

Example of a dialogue between father and son

The first line written by Learner 1, acting as the father, might be:

Father: *So there you are!*

And Learner 2, acting as the son, might respond:

Son: *Dad! I can explain!*
Father: *OK! I always enjoy your explanations!*
Son: *But Dad! It really wasn't my fault. I was . . .*
          etc.

---

3   Finally, ask volunteers to act out their dialogue to the whole class.

100 Great Activities: The Best of the Cambridge Handbooks for Language Teachers

Variations
Other ideas for bouncing dialogues

1   Parent and teenage child discussing:
     Increasing pocket money
     Bad behaviour reports from school
     Bullying

2   Famous people discussing:
     What it is like to be famous

3   Fictional characters discussing:
     The differences between their experiences and points of view

4   The learners as themselves discussing:
     Learning English
     What they would like to be doing if they were not in school
     A totally fictional exciting experience

5   The learners adopting fictitious names and characters and chatting as if they had just met for the
     first time.

98

Writing

4.4 Cinquain

From *Writing Simple Poems: Pattern poetry for language acquisition* by Vicki L. Holmes and Margaret R. Moulton

Outline	Students write five-line poems, focusing on adjectives and *-ing* forms of the verbs
Authors' comment	By creating an image without complete sentences, the cinquain (French for 'a group of five') allows students to focus on a few specific parts of speech, thereby reinforcing their understanding of grammar terms. The brevity also requires an economy of expression, emphasizing a need to refine vocabulary by selecting the best words. The use of commas to separate items in a series can also be introduced or reinforced, as can capitalization of a proper noun.
Editors' comment	Perhaps use the term *-ing* form of the verb rather than 'participle' or 'present participle' if this is the term your students are more familiar with. Ask students first to write a poem to describe someone or something they admire or love: a famous person, someone from their family, a book, a place, a painting. But, of course, it can relate to things negatively, with sometimes amusing results: things they hate or that irritate them: washing up, for example, or a villainous character from a story, book or movie.
Level	Elementary to Upper Intermediate (A2–B2)
Preparation	None

Procedure

1 Tell students that they're going to be writing a poem that creates a picture without using sentences. Instead, it uses different parts of speech and only parts of a sentence.

2 Show the students sample poems (see below). Ask them to identify the pattern by naming the parts of speech for the first three lines (noun, adjectives, present participles or *-ing* verbs). Ask them to identify the part of a sentence that makes the fourth line (*phrase*). Ask them about the last line, pointing out that the final noun is usually a *synonym* of, or a noun closely related to, the subject of the poem stated on the first line.

<table>
<tr><td align="center">Dogs</td><td align="center">Snow White</td></tr>
<tr><td align="center">Furry, cuddly</td><td align="center">Beautiful, kind</td></tr>
<tr><td align="center">Running, playing, barking</td><td align="center">Singing, dreaming, waiting</td></tr>
<tr><td align="center">Always loyal and loving</td><td align="center">Until her love arrives</td></tr>
<tr><td align="center">Friends</td><td align="center">Princess</td></tr>
</table>

Pattern

Line 1: Noun
Line 2: Two adjectives
Line 3: Three present participles / *-ing* form of the verbs
Line 4: Four-word phrase
Line 5: Synonym of noun or closely related noun

---

100 Great Activities: The Best of the Cambridge Handbooks for Language Teachers

3 Ask students to suggest one-word topics with which they are familiar. Select one to use in creating a sample poem with the class.

4 Have students brainstorm a list of adjectives related to the topic. Write down the words so they can choose from all their options. Encourage them to select the two most appropriately descriptive words to place in the second line. As you write the two words into the poem, demonstrate the use of a comma to separate two adjectives.

5 Ask students to think of present participles to describe the topic, following the same brainstorming and selection procedure used with the adjectives. As you write the three words into the poem, demonstrate the use of a comma to separate the series of three present participles.

6 Ask students for four-word phrases that describe the selected topic or how the topic affects them. Following the brainstorming and selection process, transfer the selected phrase to the poem.

7 Ask students for synonyms or words that are closely equivalent to the original topic. In our example about dogs, for instance, friend is not really a synonym for dog, but for some people it can be a close equivalent. Follow the same brainstorming and selection process as before, and then write the final line of the poem.

8 Read the completed poem aloud. Ask the students whether they want to make any changes to enhance meaning or rhythm. Allow students to negotiate changes. Edit the poem as they make suggestions and read it again.

9 Students should now be ready to begin writing their own poems as individuals, in pairs, or in small groups.

Uses
- to introduce students to each other
- to clarify understanding of an animal, maths concept, or other content-related term
- to describe a character from a story students have read
- to describe a friend, family member or pet
- to describe a place (e.g. city, state, country) or concept (e.g. home, freedom, school, love)

Variation
You might want to allow students to incorporate words from their first language within the poem.

Writing

4.5 Collective story writing

From *Teaching in Challenging Circumstances* by Chris Sowton

Outline	Students write a story collaboratively
Author's comment	This activity is particularly helpful for students who lack confidence in writing, and who remain within their safety zone. The use of anonymity encourages students to take more risks. The activity also integrates other skills (e.g. reading what classmates have written, checking for clarification). I have used this activity particularly effectively with groups in trauma settings as it provides a safe platform for exploration. Another bonus is that at the end of the session you have a huge bank of stories which you can use for future classwork – for example, language and grammar work or reading comprehensions.
Editors' comment	This is so simple yet so effective and allows full rein to the students' imaginations. It's so satisfying when the 'book' has done the full circle of the class (assuming there aren't too many students) and comes back to the student who started it: there's a real motivation to read!
Level	Pre-intermediate to Advanced (B1–C1)
Preparation	Have blank sheets of A4 paper available.

Procedure

1   Give each student a blank piece of paper. They should fold it in half, so that it looks like a book. Tell the class that they are going to write a story – but that they are going to do this collectively, not by themselves.

2   Tell students to write the name of their story at the top of their 'book'. Encourage them to be creative. Give a specific time limit (e.g. 30 seconds).

3   Tell students to give their 'book' to the person sitting next to them. They should now draw a picture (like on the front cover of the book) based on the title.

4   Now students should pass the 'book' on again. They should now write the first sentence or first short paragraph (depending on their level) of the story.

5   This can continue several more times, depending on how much time you have for the activity. By the end, you will have one story per student, but each story will have been written by many different students. These stories can then be read out. The best ones (or all of them) could be put into a class library.

Variation
Collective writing can also be done with essays, e.g. an introduction, three body paragraphs and a conclusion.

100 Great Activities: The Best of the Cambridge Handbooks for Language Teachers

4.6 Comment on the comments

From *Language Learning with Digital Video* by Ben Goldstein and Paul Driver

Outline	Students read and analyse the comments made on YouTube or other online video platforms
Authors' comment	One of the most interesting points about digital video on platforms such as YouTube are the comments that viewers leave alongside the clips themselves. These comments provide written interaction with the video and with other commentators, forming part of the multi-modal nature of these texts. This task encourages learners to both write comments about a video and anticipate and categorize other people's comments. The task is flexible, as comments are ubiquitous in many online contexts. Writing comments is an everyday occupation, but many students are pleasantly surprised by this task, which analyses these comments on a deeper level.
Editors' comment	This is a great way of practising the language of appraisal and opinion – and it could be extended to any other online forum that invites user comments, such as restaurant and hotel review sites.
Level	Elementary to Advanced (A2–C1)
Preparation	Find a video clip that has generated some controversy or divided opinion online.

Procedure

1 Briefly explain the background to your selected clip.

2 Play the clip and get learners' initial reactions. What do they think of the technique, the story, the overall effect?

3 Ask learners to anticipate the types of reaction viewers might have to the clip. They should think of both positive and negative reactions.

4 Show learners a selection of level-appropriate comments that viewers have posted about the clip. Ask them to categorize these into positive, negative or neutral. Comments could also be categorized according to the areas that they focus on. Do they refer to content, style, performances, music, concept, etc.? Were they similar to the reactions the learners had anticipated?

5 Learners discuss which comments they agree or disagree with. Are any of the comments inaccurate or too extreme? This would be a good moment to pick out key opinion adjectives to reinforce this lexical area.

6 Learners note down their own comments about the clip and their own responses to comments already there and read them out. Is there a consensus in class or are there radically differing opinions?

7 For the next class, ask learners to bring a video clip of their choice to class, together with a variety of comments to analyse.

Note

Despite the best efforts of moderators to filter offensive remarks, many such comments can still be found online. Please be aware of this when setting the task for your class.

Writing

4.7 Creative copying

From *Beginning to Write: Writing activities for elementary and intermediate learners* by Arthur Brookes and Peter Grundy

Outline	Students write their own adaptations of a well-known proverb, idiom or cliché
Authors' comment	This activity gives students an opportunity to surprise themselves with the quality of something they wrote, and thus satisfies the underlying principle of *Beginning to Write* – that early-stage learners should go far beyond using writing merely to reinforce language learning.
Editors' comment	This is in fact a dictation – but with a nice twist that gives space for students' creativity and humour. It works really well with proverbs or idioms (as in most of the examples given by the authors). Note that in the basic activity as described below, the teacher dictates which words are to be changed; but it is also possible to leave this decision open to the students – to change whichever, and however many, words they like.
Level	Pre-intermediate to Advanced (B1–C1)
Preparation	You will need to think up five or six model sentences to dictate. For example:

- I prefer <u>Sunday morning</u> to <u>Saturday night</u>.
- <u>A bird in the hand</u> is worth two <u>in the bush</u>.
- There's no <u>time</u> like <u>the present</u>.
- You can lead a <u>horse</u> to <u>water</u> but you can't make it <u>drink</u>.
- There's no place like <u>home</u>.
- <u>Variety</u> is the <u>spice</u> of life.
- Whatever <u>will be, will be</u>.
- <u>Tomorrow</u> never comes.

(See Variations below for the function of the underlined words.)

Procedure

1 Explain that you are going to dictate a number of short sentences. The students are to write down their own adapted versions. They should retain the original structure but replace one or more words or phrases in each sentence.

2 Provide an example such as 'A change is as good as a rest'. Ask the students to make suggestions for a version in which *change* and *rest* are replaced. Explain that as you dictate, the students may write down your sentence and then their own adaptation, or may write their own adaptation straight away.

3 Dictate each sentence, allowing sufficient time for most of the students to write down an adaptation.

4 After you have dictated all your sentences, allow two or three minutes for checking and for the students to write down adaptations for any sentences that they didn't complete during the dictation phase.

100 Great Activities: The Best of the Cambridge Handbooks for Language Teachers

5   Ask the students to work in small groups and select especially effective sentences to read to the rest of the class.

6   You can often make a really good wall display with the most striking sentences. Display them in prominent positions around the classroom, or publish them in a website accessible to students.

Variations

1   You can dictate and then write the sentences on the board, indicating which items should be replaced. The underlined words in the list of sentences in the examples above are suggestions for replaceable items.

2   Put students in pairs. When you dictate a sentence, indicate which words/phrases should be replaced. One student brainstorms as many words as possible to replace the first word and the other student brainstorms as many words as possible to replace the second word. So in the sentence 'a change is as good as a rest', one student would be brainstorming words to replace *change*, the other, words to replace *rest*. Then ask the students to work together and see how many good sentences they can make with the words they have brainstormed.

3   You can also use lines from poetry which can be adapted to suit the classroom itself, such as Ted Hughes's 'Through the window I see no star' (the students replace *star*). Or make up your own lines, such as 'And on the wall I dreamt there was a piece of apple pie' (the students replace 'piece of apple pie').

Writing

4.8 Delayed reverse translations

From *Translation and Own-language Activities* by Philip Kerr

Outline	Students translate an English text into their own language. They translate it back into English in a subsequent lesson, and then compare their version with the original
Author's comment	There can be few, if any, classroom activities which are so rich in learning potential and are so easily adaptable as reverse (or 'back') translation. It requires zero preparation, encourages pair or group collaboration, is highly motivating, and works equally well in monolingual and multilingual classrooms, with adults and with younger learners.
Editors' comment	This is another one of those activities that requires processing at every level: from words to sentences to whole texts. It also makes very good training for self-directed learning because it is an activity students can do on their own, at home. Whether or not they use a machine translation tool is up to them, so long as they translate the text back into English themselves.
Level	Elementary to Advanced (A2–C1)
Preparation	This activity is intended to be used in the latter part of a lesson where students have earlier read a text (e.g. for reading practice or because it contextualized a particular language item). This text might be from their coursebook, but it could also be something more authentic.
	Decide how much of the text you will ask the students to translate. For lower-level (A1 and A2) students, 40–80 words will be enough; for B1 and B2 students, 90–120 words.

Procedure

1 Towards the end of a lesson, organize the class into pairs or small groups. Ask them to look at the text or part of a text, and write a translation of it in their own language on a sheet of paper. This is collaborative work and you will need to decide if you wish to allow students to use dictionaries or other tools. Thank the students and collect their work when they have finished. If necessary, this work could be finished for homework and collected later.

2 In a subsequent lesson, ensure that the students cannot see the text which they translated in a previous lesson. Distribute the translated texts to the students who wrote them, and ask them to translate these back into English. Students will probably have queries and some will be very tempted to look at the original text. Don't answer the queries at this stage, but encourage the students to put a question mark in their translations (into English) for anything they are not sure about. Again, this is collaborative work.

3 When the students have gone as far as they can with their translations, tell them to look at the original text and to compare their version with it. Deal with any queries that arise.

105

Variations

1 Instead of using a paragraph for translation, you could also select extracts from a longer text: these might be key sentences, useful phrases or chunks of language which contain elements of grammar that you want to highlight. Remember to keep the task manageable: too much text to translate may be demotivating.

2 In the subsequent lesson, organize the class into groups of four. Instead of distributing the translated texts to the students who wrote them, distribute any two translations to each group. Using both of these texts, the group's task is to translate back into English. When they have completed this, they can compare their work with the original. They can also evaluate the two translations they worked from.

3 Instead of all the students working on the same text, select two different texts. These might be parts of a longer text which the students have read. Organize the class into pairs, and give each pair one of the texts to translate. When they have done this, reorganize the class into new pairs, where each member of the pair has translated a different text. The students work together on both translations to translate back, orally, into English, without consulting the original. Finally, they compare their work with the originals, noting any difficulties they had.

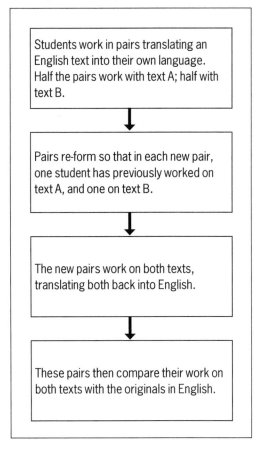

Writing

4.9 Dictogloss

From *Dictation: New methods, new possibilities* by Paul Davis and Mario Rinvolucri

Outline	Students hear a short text only once and have to jointly reconstruct it from memory
Editors' comment	This is the classic version of a very popular activity, although it has antecedents in what was once known as 'dictocomp' and also 'grammar dictation' (after the title of the book by Ruth Wajnryb published by Oxford University Press in 1990). It differs from conventional dictations in that the text that the students hear is too long to be held in short-term memory, so it has to be stored and retrieved as a 'chunk' of meaning that must then be fleshed out using the combined language resources that the students bring to bear on the task. Hence it involves processing language at every level: words, phrases, sentences and whole (albeit very short) texts.
Level	Elementary to Advanced (A2–C1)
Preparation	Choose a fairly long sentence or very short text (of not more than about 35 words) that is not too difficult relative to the language level of the group.

Procedure

1   Tell your students that you will read them the text once and once only, after which they are to jot down the main key words they can recall and set about trying to reconstruct the sentence/text in writing as accurately as they can. Read them the text.

2   The first time you do this exercise you may have to relent and allow them a second reading, as people rarely pay attention until they discover that they needed to pay attention first time round.

3   As they work at their rebuilding of the text, suggest that they get together in pairs and then fours.

4   Finally ask a 'secretary' to come out to the board to write up a final version. The secretary does not bring their script, but depends on suggestions from the group.

5   Students compare their corporate board version with your original.

Acknowledgement

This classic exercise was written up in *The English Language Teaching Journal* in 1963. It is more fully described in *Once Upon a Time*, by John Morgan and Mario Rinvolucri. See also the article by Terry Tomscha in *Practical English Teaching*.

Tomscha, T. (1983) *Practical English Teaching*. III (4 June).
Morgan, J. and M. Rinvolucri (1983) *Once Upon A Time: Using stories in the language classroom*. Cambridge University Press.
Wajnryb, R. (1990) *Grammar Dictation*. Oxford University Press.

100 Great Activities: The Best of the Cambridge Handbooks for Language Teachers

4.10 Foodies

From *Interaction Online: Creative activities for blended learning* by Lindsay Clandfield and Jill Hadfield

Outline	Students take turns posting an image of a food or drink they like / don't like and answering questions about it
Authors' comment	This is a personalized activity using an interaction pattern we call 'confetti' as it relies on a prompt from the teacher that elicits multiple responses. The activity is a universal one: taking pictures of food. It's simple to set up, but can be adapted for another topic. There is a clear language focus on food vocabulary and question forms, with error correction and reformulation built in. This activity can be done synchronously or asynchronously using a variety of platforms.
Editors' comment	This is a great way of stimulating interaction in an online setting, but it's not hard to see how it could also be adapted for classroom use: you display a picture, students 'post' questions about it – using either pen and paper or an online noticeboard tool such as Padlet or Jamboard – you collect, correct and write up the questions, then the students share pictures of food that they have on their phones and ask and answer questions about them.
Level	Beginner and above
Preparation	Take (or find) a picture of a dish or a drink that you like.

Procedure

1   Set up the task in your online platform of choice (we recommend a forum) and give it a title (e.g. Foodies). Post your picture of food or drink.

2   This is an asynchronous activity which will be done over a series of days. Post Task 1 (see below) and set a deadline for posting questions.

3   Answer students' questions as they write them. Make a note of the questions in a separate document, and correct them. When everyone has posted their questions, post Task 2 and set a deadline for posting pictures, questions and answers.

4   At the end, post a summary of all the food or drink items that were posted. Ask students to answer one of the following questions:
   - *Which was your favourite picture?*
   - *You need to plan a meal for a group of friends. What food or drink would you choose from our task?*
   - *If you could only eat two things from this week's pictures what would they be? Why?*

Task 1: Stimulus

Here is a picture I took of a (dish/food/drink/meal) I had. Everyone has to post one question about this picture. I will answer your questions. You must post your question by (*insert deadline*). You cannot repeat the same question, so pay attention to what the others have written!

108

Writing

Task 2: Interaction

Here is a list of the questions you asked about my food picture.

(*insert list of students' questions*)

I have corrected the language in some areas. For the rest of this task, you will each post a picture of food in the forum. This can be something you ate, something you like / don't like, or something you made – as long as it's food or drink!

When you have posted a picture, look at the other pictures. Post questions to at least three other people about their food picture. Use the questions in the list above to help you. If someone asks a question about your picture, post an answer. You have until (*insert deadline*) to do this task. Good luck!

Variation

This activity format can be used with many different topics, e.g. favourite item of clothing, favourite book or film, or favourite souvenir.

100 Great Activities: The Best of the Cambridge Handbooks for Language Teachers

4.11 I am...

From *Working with Images: A resource book for the language classroom* by Ben Goldstein

Outline	Students create a mental image of an object, describing it in the first person to others who have to guess what it is
Author's comment	This is a good example of an 'imaging' task, in which students work with mental images rather than physical ones. The activity is a simple one but cognitively challenging for students as it is based on the personification or embodiment of a physical object. Allowing students this kind of imaginative freedom leads to some surprising and unexpected descriptions. From the language point of view, it can be highly generative as students seek out multiple ways of describing their object from different and challenging perspectives. The task's game-like quality, with students guessing each other's objects, leads to greater motivation and engagement.
Editors' comment	This is a great way of exploiting images. The texts that the students create to describe 'themselves' could be turned into poems that are illustrated and displayed either online or on the classroom walls.
Level	Elementary (A2) and above
Preparation	Prepare a set of flashcards or digital images of objects for any lexical set you would like to cover/revise, e.g. furniture, animals, buildings, food, everyday objects.

Procedure

1 Read the text below as an example, asking students to listen and guess the object:

I'm sometimes made of plastic. I'm usually round.
I have many different shapes. But I'm often quite small.
I have numbers.
I often sit next to the bed.
You usually use me during the week.
You need me but you don't like me.

Answer: Alarm clock

2 Seat the students in groups and show different cards (or digital images) to different groups. Students work together to describe the image by imagining it in the first person. Remind them that, for their descriptions, they should consider the basic factors of material, size, shape and location before going into greater detail, as they may give too much information away too quickly.

3 Students in each group take it in turns to read out their descriptions. The other groups try to imagine what is being described.

4 Monitor to check that the descriptions correspond accurately to each image.

Writing

Variation

For higher levels, ask students to think of an object from the point of view of a Martian. Use Craig Raine's poem, *A Martian Sends a Postcard Home*, as an example. Give the class the extract from the poem below and ask them to guess the object:

In homes, a haunted apparatus sleeps,
that snores when you pick it up.
If the ghost cries, they carry it
to their lips and soothe it to sleep with sounds.
And yet, they wake it up deliberately, by tickling with a finger . . .

© Craig Raine, 1979. Used by permission of David Godwin Associates

From *100 Great Activities* © Cambridge University Press and Assessment 2024   PHOTOCOPIABLE

Answer: Telephone

Explanation: It's a machine that does not do anything (it *sleeps*) until you pick it up. The *cries* of the *ghost* are when it rings. Then you talk to it (*carry it to* [your] *lips*) or answer it and when you have finished put it back to *sleep* or hang up. We *wake it* and [tickle it] *with a finger* when we answer it or want to call someone else.

100 Great Activities: The Best of the Cambridge Handbooks for Language Teachers

4.12 I can't spell that!

From *Memory Activities for Language Learning* by Nick Bilbrough

Outline	Making spellings memorable through noticing and retrieval activities
Author's comment	I've always liked activities where learners are encouraged to identify for themselves what they want to learn, and which aren't merely a test of language items pre-determined by the teacher. This activity particularly ticks this box. There's a strong focus on learner autonomy here and we'd hope that by doing such activities in the classroom learners may be encouraged to do the same activity in their own time with their own texts.
Editors' comment	So much of teaching is about the teacher trying to pre-empt the learners making mistakes, e.g. by pre-teaching vocabulary or grammar. What we like about this activity is that it hands some of that responsibility over to the learners, and invites them to decide on what might cause difficulty performing a task.
Level	Any
Preparation	Choose a short text or dialogue to be reviewed. This could be one that has already been encountered by the learners, but which is above their active level of language.

Procedure

1 Direct the learners to the relevant page of the coursebook, or give out copies of the text. Ask them to reread the text, telling them that later you will be dictating it to them. Ask them to go through it and underline any words which they think they may spell incorrectly during the dictation stage. They now discuss these with a partner, predicting how many mistakes they think they will make.

2 The learners spend a few minutes practising the areas that they think they will have difficulties with. This may involve looking at a word, looking away and trying to rewrite it, and then looking back at the text to check.

3 They turn over the text and any papers they have used to practise on, and the teacher dictates the text whilst the learners write it out. For a greater challenge, the text can be dictated at a later point in the lesson, or even on a different day.

4 The learners look back at the original text and compare their predictions with the number of mistakes actually made. They then discuss this again in pairs.

Note

For many learners the process of thinking about mistakes that will be made is a step towards greater accuracy. The predicted number of mistakes is usually higher than the number actually made.

Writing

4.13 Letters

From *Literature in the Language Classroom* by Joanne Collie and Stephen Slater

Outline	Students write emails/letters from a character from a novel or short story
Editors' comment	You can use the opportunity to remind students of email or letter conventions: address and date (for letters), subject (for emails or formal letters), appropriate salutation and closing salutation. Note that if the literary work is well known, text generative tools, such as ChatGPT, can generate letters of this kind: so make sure your students are writing their own compositions!
Level	Pre-intermediate to Advanced (B1–C1)
Preparation	None

Procedure

1 Tell students they are going to write a letter as if they are a character from a novel or story that has recently been read by the class.

2 Students write the letter as X (one of the main characters) at the end of the novel or story to explain what happened, and how it came to happen as it did.

3 Different registers are practised by varying the people to whom the letters are to be sent (that is, X will write in a different way to their mother / wife or husband / best friend / headmaster / solicitor / boss / teacher, etc.).

4 Students read and compare corrected letters to appreciate differences of content and style.

Variation

Different characters write to each other about the events they have lived through. In Patricia Highsmith's *The Talented Mr Ripley*, for instance, half the class is Marge writing to Tom, the other half Tom writing to Marge. Letters are exchanged and, if appropriate, the activity is extended so that each person replies to the letter received.

100 Great Activities: The Best of the Cambridge Handbooks for Language Teachers

4.14 Making mine long

From *Teaching Large Multilevel Classes* by Natalie Hess

Outline	Students expand sentences by adding words and phrases
Editors' comment	This is of course easiest to do digitally: have the base sentence on the screen, and then type in the additions as students suggest them. They should do the same when working in groups, using a text program such as Word on their digital devices. As a variation, students can at any stage insert full stops and divide the text into two or more sentences.
Level	Elementary to Advanced (A2–C1)
Preparation	Write some very simple sentences that can easily be expanded. (See below for suggestions.) Have one sentence for each small group.

Procedure

1 With the whole class, demonstrate sentence expansion. For example, write the sentence *The cat likes milk* on the board and ask the class to contribute words or phrases of up to three words that would make the sentence more interesting. Students should contribute one word or phrase at a time as you or a secretary insert these words into the sentence. You could finish with a sentence that reads:

The big, gray, clever cat that belongs to my wonderful eighty-two-year-old grandmother, who lives on Eighty-Second Street in New York City on the 5th floor in a large apartment house, really and truly likes only chocolate flavoured, slightly heated, evaporated milk in the afternoon.

2 Each small group gets a sentence and expands on it.

3 Each group reads out its base sentence and its expanded sentence to the whole class.

4 A secretary from each group writes the group sentence on the board.

5 The class votes for the most original sentence. (Students are not allowed to vote for their own group.)

Suggestions for simple sentences that can be used for sentence expansion

For beginner students:	For intermediate/advanced students:
They love to eat.	The man was grateful.
The girl loved a boy.	My sister gave me a book.
My brother cooks.	Father never understood.
I can read.	He gave her a present.
I eat cake.	They met.
Pizza is good.	She enjoys movies.
He can write.	

Variation

Use base sentences from your coursebook: perhaps ones that exemplify a grammatical structure, or vocabulary, that you have recently taught.

114

Writing

4.15 Mini-stories

From *Dictionary Activities* by Cindy Leaney

Outline	Students use example sentences from a dictionary to write a story
Author's comment	I particularly like this Mini-stories activity because the example sentences in learner dictionary entries are such a rich feature. Besides illustrating the meaning of a word, example sentences provide valuable information about how the word is used, its collocations and the grammar patterns commonly associated with it. As a teacher, you can adapt the activity to your students and your aims. Happy storytelling!
Editors' comment	This is an imaginative way of using the examples in dictionary entries – which often don't get much attention. And it suggests that other 'random' sentences, such as those in a grammar reference book, could be exploited in the same way.
Level	Upper Intermediate to Advanced (B2–C1)
Preparation	Select several random example sentences from the dictionary – either print or digital. The examples below are taken from the *Cambridge Advanced Learners' Dictionary*.

Procedure

1 Write a set of example sentences from a dictionary on the board. Alternatively, ask students to look for example sentences of words that they've recently learnt.

2 Ask students to work in pairs or groups of three and use the example sentences to write a mini-story (with a beginning, a middle and an end) that makes sense.

3 An additional challenge is to use as many of the example sentences as possible.

4 Ask students to swap stories and read out another group's story. Example sentences:

> *Do you think Tim's avoiding me? I haven't seen him all day.*
> *He concocted a story about working late at the office.*
> *Bad vibes were radiating from him.*
> *Incredibly, no one was hurt in the accident.*
> *The highs and lows of life tend to average out in the end.*

Follow-up
Students select a set of example sentences to challenge other pairs or groups.

100 Great Activities: The Best of the Cambridge Handbooks for Language Teachers

4.16 Once Upon a Time

From *Extensive Reading Activities for Teaching Language* edited by Julian Bamford and Richard R. Day

Outline	Students use words from books they are reading to write their own stories
Authors' comment	This activity results in improved writing, increases in vocabulary knowledge, and insights into syntax. It also develops creativity and confidence in writing. The activity can be easily used in a variety of classroom situations (e.g. large, small), and in different contexts (ESL, EFL, multilingual). It works best with adolescents and adults.
Editors' comment	As the authors say: lots of benefits to this one! A fun variation is to put the students in small groups and tell them to compose a story – orally, no writing necessary – including as many of the words as they can. They can take turns contributing sentences, or each participant just freely suggests a continuation as they think of it. No need for any follow-up: the activity itself is motivating, and in Penny's experience results in a lot of laughter as participants suggest incongruous events in order to fit in the target words.
Level	Elementary to Advanced (A2–C1)
Preparation	Students should bring to class books that they are reading or have read.

Procedure

1 Write on the board *nouns, proper nouns, conjunctions, verbs, adjectives* and *adverbs*. The categories (parts of speech) depend on the language you are teaching.

2 Ask students for words from their books that belong in the different categories. Write these words on the board, listed under their categories. If the students are going to write a half-page story, solicit about 30 words, or as many as the students can give you in five minutes. The result is a list of random words from various stories, divided into parts of speech.

3 Tell students that they are to create their own stories from some of the words on the list. The stories all begin with the phrase *Once upon a time* or the equivalent in the target language. For a half-page story, tell students they must use at least ten words from the list; the rest of the words in their story do not have to be from the list.

4 Have the students share their stories in small groups. Afterwards, post their stories in the classroom.

Variation
Students write the stories for homework. They will either need to write down the words that are on the board, or you will need to make a handout of the words, and copy and distribute this to the students prior to the homework assignment.

Acknowledgement
Contributed by Claire Hitosugi, University of Hawaii, USA

Claire writes: 'I use this activity to help my students who are learning Japanese as a foreign language improve their writing. Students feel more comfortable writing if they use words they were previously exposed to in their reading. The activity, which I assign as homework, is an excellent way for them to be creative and develop confidence in their writing.'

Writing

4.17 Paper Talk

From *Dialogue Activities: Exploring spoken interaction in the language class* by
Nick Bilbrough

Outline	Students communicate freely with each other using notes, encouraging written activation of language through dialogue
Author's comment	This activity can be very motivating for students, particularly for those who prefer to express themselves through writing. Eventually you get a situation where everyone is involved in lots of different written conversations at the same time. Sometimes this can mean that the piles of unanswered notes start to build up, and the activity becomes difficult to draw to a close, or carries on into the break. I first encountered the idea of students passing notes to each other in *The Confidence Book* (1990) by Paul Davis and Mario Rinvolucri.
Editors' comment	The idea of interacting through text that is written in real time is what often happens with online communication and texting. But the physicality of hand-written notes adds another layer of immediacy. And, being written down, the communication is available for the teacher to mine for potential language learning opportunities. To avoid the problem of some students receiving a lot of notes and others none, you can allot each student a 'correspondent' in advance. Incidentally, the third variation below is what Scott calls 'Paper conversation', an activity he often used to start the lesson, in place of spoken chat.
Level	Any
Preparation	A stack of cut-up bits of scrap paper, some background music (optional). Arrange the classroom so that students will be able to get up from where they are sitting fairly easily.

Procedure

1   Give out a small stack of slips of paper to each student.

2   Explain that they can communicate with anyone they want to in the class. Ask them to write a short note or a question to somebody.

3   When they have finished they should get up and go over and give their note to that person. This person then replies in writing only and the process continues.

4   When everyone's understood what the activity involves, start playing the background music if you have it.

Variations

1   If everyone has access to a digital device, then this activity can be done as a texting, messaging or email exchange instead. Or, if you're using an online conferencing tool, students could use the chat option of personalized messages which only the recipient can see.

2   By taking part in the note writing yourself, you will be able to challenge learners to use particular language items, and provide feedback on what they write to you.

100 Great Activities: The Best of the Cambridge Handbooks for Language Teachers

3   Instead of getting up and giving the notes to each other, students can communicate in writing with one or both of the students on either side, by simply passing a sheet of paper between them. This way the teacher can monitor the activity, and students are left with a complete dialogue at the end which can be used for language analysis work.

4   This activity naturally lends itself to practising the language used for talking about particular things (future plans, last weekend, describing where you live, etc.) and can of course be set up to do this.

5   If you want to review language that has previously been focused on in class, write one language item on each slip of paper, before you distribute them at stage 1. The students then need to incorporate the item on the paper into whatever they write on each slip before passing on the note.

Writing

4.18 Point of view

From *Stories: Narrative activities for the language classroom* by Ruth Wajnryb

Outline	Students retell a story from the point of view of one of the characters other than the protagonist
Editors' comment	This is a great way of getting students to think 'outside the box', and to empathize with other characters rather than the conventional protagonist. (See also the activity 'Letters' on p.113.) A simpler alternative is to ask students to relate to only one scene in the story, rather than the whole thing, and describe it from the point of view of their chosen character. Note that the groups might use a 'speech to text' digital tool to write their stories, rather than writing or typing them out by hand.
Level	Pre-intermediate to Advanced (B1–C1)
Preparation	Choose a traditional fairy tale that you think your students will know, *Cinderella*, for example, or a popular folk tale from your students' culture.

Procedure

1 Write the name of the fairy tale you have chosen, e.g. *Cinderella*, on the board and elicit what students already know or remember of the story. Do this as a brainstorm and encourage students to call out words they associate with the story, for example, *ugly sisters, ball, prince, glass shoe, midnight.*

2 Tell the students that you are going to tell them the fairy tale *Cinderella*. Read out or tell the story. (If you need to, you can search for the tale online.)

3 Now read the story again, stopping to elicit suggestions from the students about particular details, for example: *What was she wearing at that time? What did the coach look like? How many people were at the ball? What kind of people were they? How did Cinderella feel when she arrived?* This draws the students into the tale, as the narrative becomes partly their collective construction.

4 After the telling, introduce the notion of *viewpoint* by asking the students who they thought was telling the story and who the narrator was most sympathetic to. If necessary, clarify the difference between the narrator being largely sympathetic to a character (as here, with Cinderella) and the story actually being written from that character's viewpoint.

5 Seat students in groups of four. Tell them that they are going to rewrite the story from the viewpoint of one of the other characters. There are five viewpoints: one of the ugly stepsisters, the fairy godmother, the prince, the stepmother and the widower. Warm students to the task by eliciting how the story might be different from the viewpoint of one of the ugly sisters.

6 To help get them started, have the groups consider the following questions about their character:
   - *How did you meet and get to know Cinderella?*
   - *What was your relationship to Cinderella?*
   - *Why did you react that way to her?*
   - *What did you want from the situation?*
   - *How do you feel about the outcomes?*

100 Great Activities: The Best of the Cambridge Handbooks for Language Teachers

7 Set the students a time limit and monitor their progress.

8 Ask each group to tell their story to the rest of the class.

Variations

1 An alternative to eliciting students' words in step 1 above is to write up the key words yourself and elicit from students what they remember about the story, as cued by the words on the board.

2 If there are more than 20 students (in groups of four), some of the viewpoints can be doubled up.

3 You might like to experiment with a non-animate narrator – for example, the story could be told from the perspective of the glass slipper or the pumpkin.

4 The final step – each group telling their story to the class – could be held over to a subsequent lesson and developed further, drawing students' attention to the ways in which the language used carries the character's particular viewpoint.

5 Other traditional fairy stories like Cinderella lend themselves to point-of-view retellings, for example:

Name of story	Possible viewpoints
Little Red Riding Hood	Little Red Riding Hood, the grandmother, the wolf, the huntsman
Goldilocks	Goldilocks, Daddy Bear, Mummy Bear, Baby Bear
Rapunzel	Rapunzel, the witch, the prince

Acknowledgement

The idea of switching perspective was suggested by Joan Novelli (1999) of Scholastic Inc. at www.findarticles.com. For an interesting article on re-thinking gender in traditional fairy tales, see Burke and Curran (2002).

Burke, E. and B. Curran (2002) 'Re-reading gender: Fairy tales and language learning', *The Language Teacher*, 26, 2, 19–23.

Writing

4.19 Running dictation

From *Communicative Activities for EAP* by Jenni Guse

Outline	Groups race to complete a text which they take turns to dictate to each other
Author's comment	It literally got my students out of their seats! This lively activity is a winner on several fronts. A welcome break from sitting at desks, it promotes communication in an energized classroom setting that caters for both weaker and stronger learners. It can be adapted to all abilities and time frames by setting it up at a word, sentence or text level. The vocabulary and grammar from the dictation provide a great base for delayed error correction/feedback or other activities. The competitiveness and teamwork that results from it makes it one of my favourite go-to activities in the classroom.
Editors' comment	This is so adaptable – to level, to topic, to text type, to target language feature – and it really does require multiple levels of processing, from spelling all the way through to textual cohesion and coherence. As a follow-up, you might like to ask the students, at a later date, if they can still recall the text well enough to reconstruct it: do this in groups and then as a whole class activity, with one student at the board acting as the class 'secretary'.
Level	Elementary to Advanced (A2–C1)
Preparation	Make a number of copies of a short text, e.g. one which contains examples of the language feature you wish to target, or any short text at the students' level.

Procedure

1 Divide the class into small groups and explain how the running dictation works. See Steps 2 to 4.

2 Around the room, attach copies of the text you have copied. There should be one copy for each group. Place each text as far away as possible from the group who will be reading it.

3 The students decide on the order that they will run to the text on the wall. The first student runs to the text, reads and memorizes a section, then runs back to the group to dictate the text. If the students have questions, or if the runner forgets part of the text, they can return as many times as they like.

4 The next runner has a turn. This continues until the complete text has been dictated.

5 Take the texts from the wall and distribute them to the groups. The students compare their texts with the original. They can then highlight the target language feature if there is one.

6 Lead a feedback session and explore these questions: *Which groups have accurately dictated the text? What were the errors in the other transcriptions? Were these errors a result of inaccurate pronunciation? What other reasons explain the errors?*

100 Great Activities: The Best of the Cambridge Handbooks for Language Teachers

4.20 Sad consequences

From *Laughing Matters* by Péter Medgyes

Outline	Students create a funny story by passing on a sheet of paper and adding events without knowing what went before
Author's comment	This activity is hoped to bring fun and laughter into the monotony of the language class by sparking witty (and bizarre) ideas from the students. While designed for pre-intermediate level, it may be re-used at intermediate+ level too, as suggested in Variations 1 and 2. This activity needs hardly any special preparation and can be thrown in by the teacher any moment when he or she feels students are beginning to flag.
Editors' comment	Walk around the class as the activity is going on to help with vocabulary or spelling (or even ideas!). You may also sometimes need to act as 'messenger', passing the folded papers across the class if some students are working faster than others.
Level	Elementary to Upper Intermediate (A2–B2)
Preparation	A blank sheet of paper for each student

Procedure

1 Each student writes down a man's name (someone famous that all the class know), followed by the word *and*, then folds the paper so that the name is hidden, and passes it on to the next student. (Note that the same folding and passing procedure is carried out in subsequent steps as well. No one is allowed to open any of the folds until the final entry has been written.)

2 The next student chooses a woman's name (again someone familiar to the class), followed by the word *met*.

3 The next student identifies the place where they met. (The preposition is *at* or *in* according to the place.)

4 The next student writes *He said* and then quotes the man.

5 The next student writes *She said* and then quotes the woman.

6 The next student provides a final consequence, beginning with *And so they*.

7 The next student unfolds the folded paper and reads out the story – which is bound to be totally absurd! To illustrate the task, you may like to write this example on the board:

Albert Einstein and Cleopatra met at a disco. He said, 'Marry me.' She said, 'Do you also like Geography?' And so they set the school on fire.

Variations

1 The same game may be based on the use of the past conditional, like this:

If Albert Einstein and Cleopatra had met at a disco, he would have said, 'Marry me.' She would have said, 'Do you also like Geography?' And so they would have set the school on fire.

2 With this game, you can also practise reported speech. In this case, instead of *He said* and *She said*, you will have *He asked if* and *She answered that*.

122

Writing

4.21 Simple selfies

From *Teaching and Developing Writing Skills* by Craig Thaine

Outline	Students read example selfie captions and practise typical expressions before writing and posting their own selfies
Author's comment	It's motivating for low-level students to do an activity that can have real-world transfer. This is a writing task that means beginner students can post something online in English. It can also be an effective way to foster group dynamics. Students work together in pairs or small selfie groups to help each other with the writing. They also get to find out about each other when they read the results of the activity.
Editors' comment	This activity not only serves as a great way to strengthen the class dynamic, but provides an authentic purpose for writing – and reading.
Level	Any
Preparation	You will need to make available to each student some example selfies with a caption of two or three sentences. You could create a worksheet with selfies about you and your life. Ask students to bring their mobile phones to class.

Procedure

1   Students look at example selfies (see below). You could ask them to match a caption to the image. Highlight any useful phrases, e.g. *Here I am ... This is me ...*

2   Put students into pairs (or threes). They take a selfie of themselves and collaboratively write a caption with two or three sentences (or two or three words or phrases, if their English is A1 level or below).

3   Put pairs together to read and compare each other's captions.

4   Students can publish the selfies on their own social media platforms. Or, if you have a class learning management system or blog, the selfies can be published there.

Worksheet

1 Match pictures 1–4 with sentences a–d.

a I love this takeaway food from the restaurant next door. It's so good.
b Here we are on holiday in Switzerland. It's really cold.
c Here I am with my son. We're playing basketball together.
d This is me in the morning. I'm thinking about my day.

2 Put the phrases together to make sentences.
a with my   here I am   friend Maria
b bicycle   my new   I love
c in the park   here we are   at the concert
d this is us   tango class   in our

3 Add sentences (i–iv) to the sentences in ex. 2.
i I love this music.
ii It's a difficult dance!
iii We're having coffee and cake.
iv It's easy to ride.

From *100 Great Activities* © Cambridge University Press and Assessment 2024   PHOTOCOPIABLE

Writing

4.22 Summarising the summary

From *Literature in the Language Classroom* by Joanne Collie and Stephen Slater

Outline	Students summarize a text, then summarize the summary more briefly
Editors' comment	You can do this with almost any text. Note that it would be very easy to get an AI generative text tool such as ChatGPT to do the summaries as suggested in this activity. So do it in class rather than through online correspondence, and make sure the students are indeed working out their own summaries. You might later, for fun, show in class how an AI generative text tool did the same tasks, and compare with students' versions.
Level	Pre-intermediate to Advanced (B1–C1)
Preparation	A text which the students have studied

Procedure

1 Students are divided into three groups (or two or three sets of three groups if you have a large class). Each writes a summary of the section of a text the class has recently read, with a maximum number of words, for example, 70.

2 They then pass on their summary to the next group, which must reduce it to half its length, that is, to 35 words.

3 This is now passed on to the third group, which halves the length again, to 17 words. Each group is thus involved in reducing all three summaries.

4 Final versions are read out and changes discussed.

100 Great Activities: The Best of the Cambridge Handbooks for Language Teachers

4.23 Thoughts

From *Using Newspapers in the Classroom* by Paul Sanderson

Outline	Students imagine what people depicted in photographs might be thinking
Editors' comment	Pictures are always an excellent basis for imaginative language work: see also Alan Maley's 'Becoming a picture' (p.12). Pictures of people as described here can be downloaded from online sources or from your own collections; alternatively use digital tools that create pictures from a written description.
Level	Elementary to Upper Intermediate (A2–B2)
Preparation	Prepare a number of dramatic photographs of people with unusual or interesting expressions on their faces, or who are in strange positions or situations. Print out each onto a separate sheet of paper, or save as a digital document with space to write below.

Procedure

1 To demonstrate the activity, show your students one of the photographs and ask them to imagine what the person in the photograph might be thinking at that moment. Your students will usually come up with some amusing suggestions, and you should write all their ideas on the board.

2 a. Using paper: display all the other photograph sheets around the room and explain to your students that they should study the people in the photographs carefully – how they are standing, what they are doing and, in particular, the expressions on their faces. They should then write what they imagine the person in each photograph might be thinking at that moment. When they have decided, they should write this on the sheet. They should do this for all the photographs, making sure that they do not repeat any other student's ideas.

  b. Using digital tools: display the pictures on a noticeboard such as Jamboard or Padlet, allowing plenty of space for students to add text underneath each of them. Students add their ideas on the person's thoughts for as many of the pictures as they can.

3 When all the photos have several contributions, stop this writing stage and ask your students to read each other's ideas.

4 Finally, with the whole class, discuss and comment on the most imaginative and amusing thoughts they wrote.

Follow-up

If the photograph is associated with a newspaper article or website, keep the accompanying text and make a note of which photograph each corresponds to. Display all the text next to their corresponding photographs, and ask your students to read them. Ask your students to comment on whether they think the photographs are appropriate for the articles they accompany, and whether the thoughts they wrote are appropriate for the original context.

5 Vocabulary

The importance of learning and reviewing vocabulary can hardly be overestimated; and the activities in this section provide opportunities both for vocabulary expansion ('Looking up words you know' or 'Input enhancement') and for meaningful repetition and consolidation ('Do you remember?', 'A long and growing list'). Sometimes the tasks require encountering or using the vocabulary in context ('Search a page', 'Connect two'), sometimes they focus on single items ('How many things can you think of that … ?' and 'Pass it round'). Often the tasks suggested involve thinking 'outside the box': the 'Odd one out' activity, for example, does not dictate in advance which is the 'right' answer, but challenges students to find different right answers and justify them. But all of the activities provide opportunities for intensive, as well as enjoyable, engagement with English vocabulary.

100 Great Activities: The Best of the Cambridge Handbooks for Language Teachers

5.1 A long and growing list

From *Games for Language Learning 3rd edition* by Andrew Wright, David Betteridge and Michael Buckby

Outline	Each student repeats what the person before said and adds something, so the utterances get longer
Authors' comment	Whatever sentence pattern you choose (see Variations), the challenge of this game is to remember and repeat all the additions given earlier and then to contribute your own. The object of all the variations of the game is to see how long and elaborate a sentence learners can devise. You might judge that your learners cannot do such a game spontaneously and will need preparation time, perhaps in groups, using dictionaries or textbooks as necessary. In some of the alternative sentence patterns and stipulated rules it might be essential for this preparation to be done and, in any case, preparation then involves everybody.
Editors' comment	This is a classic, and excellent for younger classes. As the lists get longer and longer, you will find that other members of the class are helping the student whose turn it is to remember all the items – this is good, it keeps everyone involved and lowers the stress for the student trying to remember. But anyway, stop and start again if you see that the list is becoming unmanageable.
Level	Beginner to Elementary (A1–A2)
Preparation	None

Procedure

1 Seat the learners in a circle (or two or three circles if it is a big class).

2 Tell the learners that, in this game, a given sentence pattern – *I went shopping and I bought . . .* – must be completed by adding any words that make sense, each player adding one more item to the list when it is their turn. Each player must repeat whatever has been said by the previous player before making an addition to the list. For example:

Learner 1: *I went shopping and I bought a shirt.*
Learner 2: *I went shopping and I bought a shirt and a skirt.*
Learner 3: *I went shopping and I bought a shirt, a skirt and a sausage.*
Learner 4: *I went shopping and I bought a shirt, a skirt, a sausage and an apple.*
Learner 5: *I went shopping and I bought a shirt, a skirt, a sausage, an apple and a car.*

3 Also explain that each player must act out or mime, however cursorily, each of the items referred to, while speaking. The rest of the class (or group, if the game is based on group organization) might also mime at the same time. Encourage creative and humorous ideas!

128

Vocabulary

Variations

This game may be played using other sentence patterns which allow learners to focus on different types of vocabulary and grammar points, for example:

- *The teacher's cat is very old, rather fat, bald with a long beard . . .* (any adjectives and adjectival phrases)
- *The teacher's cat is an active cat and a bad cat and a cute cat . . .* (adjectives in alphabetical order plus *a/an*)
- *This morning I bought a brown bag . . .* (noun and adjective with the same initial letter)
- *Kirsty has an elephant, Tom has a monkey, David has a python, and I have an armadillo . . .* (*have/has* plus animals and *a/an*)
- *This morning, before six o'clock, I swam across the lake, and I read Shakespeare, and I argued with my neighbour, and I . . .* (simple past tense)

5.2 Association webs

From *Using the Board in the Language Classroom* by Jeannine Dobbs

Outline Brainstorming words associated with a central theme
Editors' comment This is based on the 'sun-ray' activity, used by many teachers, but with the addition of further links using secondary words as a focus. Feel free to add a few further words that the students don't know yet, explaining what they mean and what their connection is with the central word: it's a good opportunity to teach new items, linking them to ones they already know.
Level Beginner to Intermediate (A1–B1+)
Preparation None

Procedure
1 In the centre of a large expanse of board, write a word that students are learning or one that is a key word in content they are studying. Draw a circle around the word.
2 Ask students to tell you words that they associate with the central word. Write these words around the central word, circle each one, and link it to the central word by a line.
3 Now invite students to add secondary items to the words around 'Weather'. For example, they might attach 'snow/snowy' to 'cold', or 'heat wave' to 'hot'.

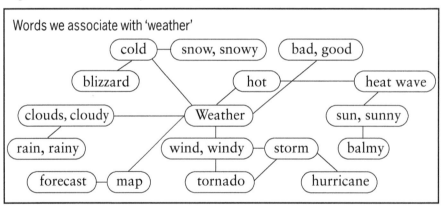

Variations
1 Using different-coloured chalk or markers to circle or underline the different parts of speech can be effective.
2 If the central word is a noun, ask students to give you adjectives that go with it, verbs it could act upon, or verbs that could act upon it.
3 If the central word is a verb, ask students to give you adverbs that go with it, nouns that could be its subjects, and nouns that could be its objects (if the verb is transitive).
4 Ask students to give you words that begin with the same letter or with the same sound as the central word.

Vocabulary

5 Ask students to give you words of the same 'class' (e.g. synonyms / words of similar meaning, or words that follow a similar spelling pattern).

6 Give students a superordinate as the central word and ask them to give you subordinates (e.g. animal: horse, cat, elephant).

100 Great Activities: The Best of the Cambridge Handbooks for Language Teachers

5.3 Connect two

From *Vocabulary Activities* by Penny Ur

Outline	Students make up sentences that include two of the items from a list
Author's comment	The conventional way of reviewing vocabulary is to ask students to compose contextualizing sentences: one sentence for each word. When you ask them to contextualize two of them in a single sentence, it becomes more challenging. The challenge is rooted in the fact that this task activates higher-order thinking skills – as do the ones suggested in Variation 2 below. All things being equal, a task based on higher-order thinking skills – connecting, applying, exemplifying, generalizing, evaluating, distinguishing between true and false and so on – will be more interesting than one based on lower-order thinking such as identifying or recalling.
Editors' comment	The activity encourages a perfect balance of conformity (i.e. being true to the meanings and grammatical behaviour of the chosen words) and creativity (i.e. combining the words in original and likely memorable ways) – you can't ask much more for a language practice activity!
Level	Any
Preparation	Select 10 to 15 vocabulary items you want to review.

Procedure

1 Write or display on the board a set of 10 to 15 items you want to review, in a 'scatter' (not vertical lists or horizontal lines). The items can include both words and multi-word expressions.

2 Invite students to volunteer any sentence they like that contextualizes any two of the items.

3 For the sentence that the student gives, draw a line on the board that connects the two items.

4 Continue until every item has been connected to at least one other. (You'll find that some students soon start creating sentences that link three or more items: that's fine.)

Follow-up
Point to a line, and ask students to recall what the sentence was that it represents. Delete that line. Carry on until all the lines have been deleted.

Variations
Other ways of making sentence contextualizing of the target items more interesting are:
• Make up sentences that are clearly true.
• Make up questions to which you don't know the answer.
• Make up sentences that are clearly false.
• Make up negative sentences (i.e. that include *not, never* etc.).
• Make up personalized true statements beginning with *I*.

132

Vocabulary

5.4 Desirable qualities

From *Personalizing Language Learning* by Griff Griffiths and Kathy Keohane

Outline	Students talk about personal qualities
Editors' comment	You might start off this activity by asking students to brainstorm all the personal qualities they know, both positive and negative. Then add a few more they didn't know, explaining them as you go – an excellent opportunity to teach more vocabulary. Note that you can expand this initial list to include other kinds of attributes that are not exactly personal qualities: *rich* or *poor*, for example. And later another interesting variation might be to ask students which qualities they think are important (or to be avoided!) for different professions or functions: for a teacher, for example, or a bus driver, or a parent.
Level	Elementary to Advanced (A2–C1)
Preparation	None

Procedure

1 Read out the set of adjectives for the level you are working with (there are ready-to-use sets below) and ask learners to raise their hands to indicate whether they consider it a positive quality. As you are doing so, check that everyone understands the meaning of all of them, and clarify any possible ambiguities (e.g. *thoughtful* – to describe someone who likes thinking, or someone who is considerate?).

2 Write the adjectives on the board.

3 Ask learners to choose the four words from their set that they would most like to apply to themselves, and to rank them in order of importance from 1 to 4, 1 being the most important. An elementary result might look like this:

4 Now ask them to write down and put a cross next to any words they would not wish to apply to themselves. Again, an intermediate result might look like this:

```
greedy    x
boring    x
careless  x
shy       x
nasty     x
```

5 Now ask the class to choose from the same set the four features they would most wish for in a friend. Again, ask everyone to rank these, this time using letters a–d in order of importance, 'a' being the most important, and to write down and draw a circle next to the qualities they would not like their friend to have. For example:

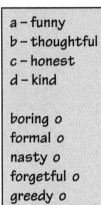

6 Ask learners to work with a partner and to compare their opinions, giving reasons.

> **Examples of qualities**
>
> Elementary to Intermediate adjectives
>
> friendly, cheerful, greedy, calm, kind, loving, funny, gentle, thoughtful, boring, formal, nasty, brave, generous, wise, helpful, forgetful, careless, honest, shy, strong
>
> Intermediate to Upper Intermediate adjectives
>
> sociable, approachable, relaxed, ambitious, deep, blunt, respectful, determined, selfish, distant, uptight, nervous, self-conscious, uninspiring, quarrelsome, amusing, straightforward, responsible, rough, proud, charming
>
> Upper Intermediate to Advanced adjectives
>
> cultured, witty, sneaky, driven, antagonistic, sly, pedantic, shallow, charitable, highly strung, nonconformist, aggressive, compassionate, altruistic, sharp, ambitious, approachable, controlled, upstanding, self-confident, narrow-minded, passionate

Vocabulary

5.5 Do you remember?

From *Using the Board in the Language Classroom* by Jeannine Dobbs

Outline	Students try to recall a set of words they have memorized from a list on the board
Editors' comment	This is a favourite of Penny's: very quick to do and an effective review of vocabulary and spelling. She always uses the variation suggested by the author below: getting students to share and help each other remember before revealing the answers. You'll notice that when students have recalled and written down all they can on their own, they start looking up at the ceiling, so when you see a lot of the students doing this, it's a signal that you can move on to the next stage!
Level	Beginner to Intermediate (A1–B1+)
Preparation	Select a set of words you have recently taught.

Procedure

1   On the board, write or display 10 or 12 vocabulary words your class has been working on.

2   Give students a few minutes to look over the list, and then erase or hide it.

3   Ask students (at their desks) to write down all the words they can remember. (Spelling counts!)

4   After a few minutes, rewrite or reveal the list so that students can check and correct or add missing words if necessary.

Variation
Before the final step of revealing the list, have students collaborate in pairs or groups of three to try to remember more of the words and make a combined list.

100 Great Activities: The Best of the Cambridge Handbooks for Language Teachers

5.6 Guess them fast!

From *Vocabulary Activities* by Penny Ur

Outline	Students get other students to guess words by providing hints
Author's comment	The 'beat the clock' element here is really important, and increases the number of hints the students give and the rate at which they do so. Without it, the process can become tedious and even grind to a halt. In any case, don't insist on the guesser guessing every single item: if you see they are stuck, tell them what it is and move on.
Editors' comment	This is a popular review activity. It can be done at the end of the lesson to review words that have been taught earlier, or at the beginning of the next lesson. The words do not, in this case, necessarily have to belong to the same lexical set.
Level	Beginner to Elementary (A1–A2) (or higher, see Variation 2)
Preparation	Sets of words to be projected onto the board, or written up, whose members all belong to the same category. You can use the ones shown below or ones you prepare yourself that include items you want to review.

Procedure

1   Ask one student to come to the front of the class and face the class with their back to the board.

2   Display five words on the board:

   a mango   a banana   an apple   a lemon   a pineapple

3   Tell the rest of the class they have one minute (or two, or whatever time you decide) to get the student to guess all five items. They can say what the general category is (*fruit* in this case), and may give any hints they like, but only based on meanings (they may not say 'it begins with *b*', for example). They may start only when you say 'Go'. The student may not ask questions.

4   Say 'Go'. Time them, and stop them after the time limit even if the student has not guessed everything.

5   If you're not sure they've got the idea, do this again, with another student and a different set of fruits:

   a pear   a plum   grapes   an orange   a coconut

6   Divide the class into two teams. The first team sends a representative to stand with their back to the board. You write up a set of items (see below for some possibilities) and the team tries to get their representative to guess what they are within the set time. Then the process is repeated with the other team, using the next set of items. Meanwhile, you make sure they keep to the allotted time limit, and write up the scores: the current team scores a point for every word successfully guessed in the time.

Variations

1   Get two students, rather than one, to stand with their backs to the board each time. This is less stressful and enables you to activate more students as guessers.

136

Vocabulary

2   You can do the same with higher levels, even academic classes, using categories such as homes, equipment, subjects of study, abstract nouns, abstract verbs, terminology from a particular field.

3   Reverse the teacher–student functions: ask students to write five words or phrases you have recently taught them on the board while you have your back to it; then they give you hints and you try to guess what they are.

Example categories
Beginner to Elementary (A1–A2)

Colours		Actions	
Team 1	Team 2	Team 1	Team 2
green	red	walk	run
yellow	blue	drink	eat
black	white	look	listen
brown	orange	speak	write
grey	purple	read	think

Pre-intermediate to Intermediate (B1–B1+)

Professions		Feelings	
Team 1	Team 2	Team 1	Team 2
soldier	gardener	disappointment	hope
chemist	detective	fear	relief
social worker	pilot	joy	pity
journalist	actor	anger	regret
firefighter	secretary	jealousy	excitement

Upper Intermediate to Advanced (B2–C1)

Tools		Verbs	
Team 1	Team 2	Team 1	Team 2
screwdriver	hoe	demonstrate	investigate
hammer	sword	broadcast	implement
scalpel	lasso	neutralize	optimize
needle	nailfile	specify	monitor
ladle	forceps	enforce	facilitate

100 Great Activities: The Best of the Cambridge Handbooks for Language Teachers

5.7 How many things can you think of that . . . ?

From *Five-Minute Activities: A resource book of short activities* by Penny Ur and Andrew Wright

Outline	Students brainstorm ideas for things that accord with a brief description
Authors' comment	This is a vocabulary review exercise with a game-like challenge. As it stands, it targets pre-advanced students, but can be adapted for advanced and even academic ones: all the terms that relate to the heart, for example (for medical students), or all the adjectives that could apply to the word *research*. But make sure that whatever criterion you use, it relates to the meaning of the word, not the form: a task based on form (words beginning with *c*, for example) is less useful.
Editors' comment	Any activity that requires students to 'dig around' in their lexical store is good for vocabulary reinforcement: the more times we retrieve an item from the store, the better chance it has of being remembered, and of being available for productive use. This activity works on this principle and, because it is collaborative, it takes some of the stress out of brainstorming.
Level	Elementary to Pre-intermediate (A2–B1)
Preparation	None

Procedure

1 Students try to think of and note down as many things as they can that fit a given definition and that they know in English. For instance, you might tell them to think of as many items as they can that are small enough to fit into a matchbox (see below for some more ideas).

2 Pool all the ideas on the board as they are suggested. Alternatively, divide the class into groups and have a competition to see which group can think of the most items.

How many things can you think of that . . . ?

. . . are bigger than you are?

. . . are rectangular?

. . . are round?

. . . are long and thin?

. . . make a noise?

. . . work on electricity?

. . . are made of paper/wood/glass?

. . . people enjoy looking at?

. . . have handles?

. . . you can use to sit on?

Vocabulary

5.8 Input enhancement

From *Lexical Grammar: Activities for teaching chunks and exploring patterns* by Leo Selivan

Outline	After reading a text containing highlighted multi-word expressions (chunks), students turn over the text and try to recall them
Author's comment	Input enhancement can be used with any level and is easy to set up. Although not conclusive, research suggests that input enhancement is more effective when accompanied by an explicit instruction to learners to notice the highlighted items. It might therefore be a good idea to tell learners in advance – before reading – to pay attention to the highlighted chunks. Of course, the question remains: how do you select chunks that are worth attention? Your own intuition will play a part, along with recourse to good dictionaries and online corpora.
Editors' comment	This activity gets round the problem of learners not being easily able to identify lexical chunks in a text. Instead, the chunks are identified for them, and their job is to try and recall them – the first stage in being able to internalize them. The versatility of this activity – in terms of level, text type, language focus – makes it especially useful. And you don't need to print the text: you can simply project it, allow learners time to study it, and then remove it.
Level	Elementary to Advanced (A2–C1)
Preparation	Choose a short text from the materials you are using or from the internet (ensuring it is copyright free). Highlight around 8 to 12 chunks in the text (see below for an example). Then print enough copies for the class (one per learner). You can even use different colours for different chunks, especially if the text is displayed on a screen.

Procedure

1 Distribute copies of the highlighted text (or project on-screen), asking learners to read it straight away. Set a time limit of around two minutes.

2 Immediately after learners finish reading, ask them to turn the page over and write down as many of the highlighted chunks as they can remember.

3 Learners can compare answers in pairs or move around the room to complete their lists with the help of other students.

4 Conduct feedback, eliciting the contexts in which the target chunks were used.

5 Proceed to other post-reading activities, such as a comprehension check or discussion questions.

100 Great Activities: The Best of the Cambridge Handbooks for Language Teachers

Example text

United Parcel Service

With the help of UPS, you can have a parcel sent quickly to almost anywhere at any time. The company was founded at the beginning of the twentieth century. It was a time when more and more businesses and private individuals needed to get errands done and messages delivered. UPS founder, James Casey, saw a business opportunity, so he borrowed $100 to set up his own business, Most deliveries were made on foot or by bicycle. Today UPS delivers 16 million packages and documents a day by airplane, ship and truck. One important condition for the new UPS franchise owners is that they have to be good in English and have to pass an exam to prove it.

Acknowledgement

Text with highlighted chunks from:

Helliwell, M. (2015) *Business Plus Level 3: Preparing for the workplace.* Cambridge University Press.

Vocabulary

5.9 Looking up words you know

From *Planning Lessons and Courses: Designing sequences of work for the language classroom* by Tessa Woodward

Outline	Learning more about known words by looking them up in a dictionary
Author's comment	Whether our students use online or paper-based dictionaries, some may not realise the wealth of information available in these resources. Others might feel daunted by these large treasure troves and need gentle coaxing to turn to them and use them with any confidence. And many students, especially at elementary level, would rather use a bilingual dictionary than an English to English one which, as they progress in their vocabulary acquisition, will prove more and more useful. The activity below is a non-threatening way into monolingual dictionary use.
Editors' comment	Looking up words you know is, as the author says, an unthreatening but very enriching vocabulary activity. Apart from new meanings, learners can often find new collocations, or useful phrases that include the target item. We wouldn't limit to finding one thing they didn't know before, but rather 'find at least one thing, and more if you can'! And you can do the same with a thesaurus: look up a word to find lots of other associated words or phrases, or opposites.
Level	Beginner to Upper Intermediate (A1–B1+)
Preparation	None

Procedure

1 Ask students to look up words that are either:
   a) international, e.g. 'Coke' or 'Cola' or 'café'
      or
   b) false friends, that is, the sound and/or spelling is the same or very similar in both the mother tongue and target language but the meaning is different, e.g. 'aktuel'/'actually', 'simpatico'/'sympathetic', 'demander'/'demand'
      or
   c) ones students are sure they know in the target language, e.g. 'table' or 'chair'.

2 Whichever category you choose, ask students to look the words up and tell you one thing about them that they didn't know beforehand. The thing they choose may be semantic, phonemic, syntactic or relating to usage. They are in fact almost guaranteed to find out something new and interesting about the word they look up, such as that *coke* is a name for the drug cocaine, that false friends are no friends at all, or that *chairs* can be jobs at a university.

100 Great Activities: The Best of the Cambridge Handbooks for Language Teachers

5.10 Odd one out

From *CLIL Activities: A resource for subject and language teachers* by Liz Dale and Rosie Tanner

Outline	Students discuss which word or picture is the odd one out
Authors' comment	This activity is quick and easy to design and exemplary for CLIL. Teachers appreciate how easy it is to find suitable words for this task in any coursebook. They quickly see how the activity helps make visible students' understanding of both important subject concepts and language. Students enjoy coming up with alternative reasoning for why a word is the odd one out, and teachers enjoy hearing all the options they come up with. The activity can be used with all subjects, group sizes and in online break-out rooms. It also works equally well with non-specialist vocabulary in EFL classes.
Editors' comment	What we like about 'odd one out' activities like this one, is that there is no 'right answer', which allows for lots of discussion within groups and comparison across groups. It also makes the activity more challenging and fun than the conventional 'odd one out' activities which have one obvious right answer, and produces longer and more interesting discussions and more engagement with the target items.
Level	Elementary to Advanced (A2–C1)
Preparation	Skim through a unit in your coursebook. Select groups of four words/concepts/ideas that come from the same domain (e.g. *ocean, river, lake, glacier* or *emancipation, segregation, integration, assimilation*). There should not be an obvious odd one out in your groups of four, but several possibilities. Make a table like the example below for each group of four words. You will need a copy of the table for each group of three learners.

Procedure

1   Write four words on the board. Discuss with the class which word could be the odd one out and why. Encourage the learners to think creatively and to come up with a variety of reasons. These might be to do with meaning, colour, number of letters, pronunciation, etc.

2   Divide the class into groups of three. Give each group a copy of the table you prepared (see example below).

3   Ask the learners to circle the word they feel is the odd one out in each set and to write their reason in the final column.

4   Ask the groups in turn to explain some of their choices to a partner or the rest of the class.

Set					Reason
1	flow	basin	course	source	
2	spring	rainfall	flow	hail	
3	ocean	river	lake	glacier	
4	freshwater	groundwater	salt water	glacier	
5	volcano	earthquake	tsunami	flood	

From *100 Great Activities* © Cambridge University Press and Assessment 2024   PHOTOCOPIABLE

Vocabulary

Follow-up
Create similar tables for students to work on in later lessons, based on concepts from topics or sub-topics of the course. Students could also create their own tables to try out on each other.

Variation
Challenge the groups to find reasons to identify each word in any set as the odd one out.

Acknowledgement
This activity is adapted from:
Leat, D. (2001) *Thinking Through Geography*, Cambridge: Chris Kington Publishing.

5.11 Pass it round

From *Vocabulary Activities* by Penny Ur

Outline Students pass round a sheet of paper with a basic cue or question and add possible responses

Author's comment 'Pass it round' is a lovely collaborative technique, here used to expand vocabulary, but can be used for all sorts of other purposes. For example: constructing stories (each individual adds another sentence before passing on: see 'Collective story writing' on p.101) or poems (each adds a new line), adding responses to feedback questionnaires, and more. It's a way of getting students to teach and learn from each other, and leads to a lot of participation.

Editors' comment As in all brainstorming activities, this requires learners to retrieve words (and collocations) from memory: a key process in word learning. The collaborative element reduces anxiety, while the time limit adds just the right amount of urgency. We can see this being developed into a game, with team members taking turns at the board to see which team can come up with the most words in the time limit.

Level Elementary to Advanced (A2–C1)

Preparation Prepare enough sheets of paper so that each group of three can get a different one, with cues as shown below.

Procedure

1 Write on the board a base expression like:
   You can break...

2 Invite students to suggest what objects might come after this, and add them like this:

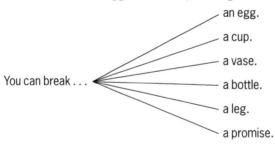

3 Divide the class into groups of three, and give each a sheet of paper with a different beginning phrase. Here are some possibilities:

You can eat...	You can sit on...
You can listen to...	You can build...
You can watch...	You can read...
You can cut...	You can write...
You can enjoy...	You can talk about...
You can love...	You can learn...
You can hold...	

Vocabulary

4   Tell students they have three minutes to fill in as many possible objects as they can. After three minutes, ring a bell, or call out *Stop!* and tell them to pass the sheet of paper to another group.

5   Each group now works on its new paper for three minutes: they have to read what the previous group has written and add more.

6   The process continues; make sure that each sheet of paper moves each time to a group which hasn't seen it before.

7   Move round the classroom helping groups think of new items; teach new words as necessary.

8   When all groups have contributed, students should leave the finished sheets on their desks and move round the class to read all the others.

9   Take in the sheets, and then either a), read out the results immediately, stopping to teach or review any items that some or all of the class don't know or b), take the lists home and the next day go over any of the items you think the class may not have known, or need to review.

Variations

1   With younger learners, tell each group to use a different-coloured pen or pencil. This way they can easily identify, when the activity is over, which group contributed what to each sheet.

2   Use negative instead of positive base expressions: *You can't eat . . .* etc.

3   Use combinations other than verb + object. For example, provide a verb and the groups add adverbs: *We can talk . . .ly.* Or provide a noun, and they suggest adjectives: *a(n) . . . dog.* Or provide an adjective, and they supply nouns: *a blue . . . .*

100 Great Activities: The Best of the Cambridge Handbooks for Language Teachers

5.12 Search a page

From *Vocabulary Activities* by Penny Ur

Outline	Students locate the target items in a page of text
Author's comment	This activity is not only a vocabulary review exercise: it also practises the skill of scanning, and indirectly reviews the content of the text as a whole. It can, however, get tedious if it goes on for very long: which is why I've limited the number of items to be found to ten. Though you can, of course, do the same thing again, with the same text but different items, in another lesson.
Editors' comment	This is a great way of reinforcing the vocabulary learning opportunities offered by a text. It's also a way of getting the most out of a text – and you can imagine the activity being extended to searching the text for grammatical items – an irregular verb, an adverb, a preposition of time . . . .
Level	Beginner to Intermediate (A1–B1+)
Preparation	None

Procedure

1 Tell students to look at a reading text they have recently been working on and from which you have taught some new vocabulary items. The text can be either print or digital.

2 Call out one of the items and challenge students to find it in the text. Students raise their hands as they find it, and may underline or highlight the sentence or phrase in which it occurs in the text.

3 When you see more than half the students have raised their hands, go on to the next item. Reassure the students that it doesn't matter if not all of them find all the items at this stage; you'll show them all of them later.

4 When you have been through seven to ten items, stop.

5 Call out each item again, but this time a student who found it says where it is (easier if your text provides line numbers), and reads out the immediate context: the sentence or phrase within which the item appears. Students who didn't find it before can now locate it; help them where necessary.

Variations

1 Students take turns locating and calling out an item instead of you doing so. In this case you too have to search for and underline it!

2 If you have a monolingual class whose language you know, call out the L1 translation of the target items: students find the English equivalents in the text.

6 Grammar

The activities in this section typically target a specific grammatical feature, and then give the learners opportunities to engage with it through an interesting task that involves conveying (written or spoken) meanings. Sometimes this means communicative interaction ('Question stories'); sometimes just playful suggestions ('Oh!'). In any case, they make a welcome break from the routine gapfills and transformation exercises normally provided in coursebooks and online grammar practice. You'll find that most of the activities can be adapted to practise features other than the one focused on in the original; and others, for example 'Sentence repetition' or 'Student-generated test', you can use for any grammatical structure(s) you like!

100 Great Activities: The Best of the Cambridge Handbooks for Language Teachers

6.1 Adjectives on the internet

From *Grammar Practice Activities: A practical guide for teachers* by Penny Ur

Outline	Students search online for interesting contexts for a given grammatical form
Author's comment	This activity was designed to practise the comparative of adjectives: but actually it can be used for almost any vocabulary item or grammatical form you like. The goal is to find a context for the target bit of language that is understood by students, and fun. An alternative would be to ask an AI generative text tool such as ChatGPT to create seven sentence contexts for the target bit of language, and then choose the most interesting.
Editors' comment	This is a simple but effective use of the vast resources of the internet for language study. And once students become accustomed to searching the internet for examples, it's not a huge step to introduce them to online corpus tools, where they can refine their searches, e.g. by searching for examples from academic writing, from conversation or from movies.
Level	Elementary to Pre-intermediate (A1–B1)
Preparation	None

Procedure

1   Brainstorm as many adjectives as the class can think of (up to about 30), and write them on the board.

2   Each student selects one of them and writes down its comparative form.

3   They search online for this form and find five different contexts in which it is used. These must be a) clearly understood and b) interesting or funny.

4   Each student presents his/her most interesting example. Who has found the funniest or most original contexts?

Variation

Do the same with the superlative form.

Note

1   It's fine for two or more students to choose the same adjective if you don't have enough to go round. The results are likely to be different anyway.

2   The students can do this on their own digital devices in class, or at home, bringing the results to the next lesson.

Grammar

6.2 Circle comparisons

From *Grammar Practice Activities: A practical guide for teachers* by Penny Ur

Outline	Students suggest comparisons between any of the items shown on the board
Author's comment	The advantages of this activity are that there is virtually no preparation, but a lot of practice of the target grammar based on a visual focus. The fact that students can suggest whatever they like means that often they come up with original or amusing ideas, so it's also fun.
Editors' comment	For higher-level students, the comparison language could be more elaborated, e.g. *X is not as* [adjective] *as Y; X is not the same as Y because* . . . ; *One difference between X and Y is* . . . , etc.
Level	Beginner to Elementary (A1–A2)
Preparation	None

Procedure

1 On the board, write or display several nouns laid out in a rough circle as follows:

pasta

salt   apples

yoghurt   ice cream

water   fish

curry

The nouns should be connected in sense to a common theme (see below for more examples).

2 Ask students to suggest a point of comparison between any two. For example:

Ice cream is sweeter than salt.

3 Draw a line between 'ice cream' and 'salt' to represent the link, and ask for another sentence linking two other items, and so on, until there is a criss-cross of lines linking the words.

Follow-up

1 Point to one of the lines, and challenge the class to remember what sentence it represented. If they succeed, delete the line. Continue until all the lines are deleted.

2 For homework, students may be given sets of nouns on paper to work on individually, drawing in the lines and writing the corresponding sentences below.

Variation

1 Ask the students to suggest the original eight items themselves, rather than deciding on them yourself. Give them a basic topic, and ask them to suggest nouns: food, as here, or animals, professions, objects, types of home, machines, vehicles, clothes . . . .

2 Ask the students to say which is *the* . . . *-est* or *the most* . . . of all the items in the circle. Draw a circle round the item they have selected. Go on until all the items have been circled (if possible!); it's OK to circle some items more than once.

100 Great Activities: The Best of the Cambridge Handbooks for Language Teachers

6.3 Drawing my natural world

From *Five-minute Activities for Young Learners* by Penny McKay and Jenni Guse

Outline	Students work in groups in a race to guess a sentence that one of the students draws
Authors' comment	This activity engages all students in a small group drawing activity which integrates reading, speaking, and the revision of previously taught language items – in this case, prepositions of place, present continuous tense, and vocabulary from the natural world. The activity is versatile because the teacher can construct the sentences so that they reflect the vocabulary that is currently being covered in the curriculum. It retains the students' interest because most children love to draw and outdoor activities always appeal.
Editors' comment	This is an activity Scott has done again and again with a teens class and they really got into it. Once the 'game' part of the activity is over, you can elicit the sentences back from the students (they have their drawings to prompt their memories) and write them on the board. The sentences can then become the focus of a language review.
Level	Beginner to Upper Intermediate (A1–B2)
Preparation	Prepare some sentences that all share the same structure and theme – in the example below, it's the natural world. Copy each sentence on to a separate card, making sure it is easily legible.

Procedure

1 Divide the class into groups with three children in each group.

2 Ask one child from each group to come to the front of the class, and show them one of the sentences. Each child should see the same sentence clue.

3 They return to their groups and, without speaking, draw the information you have shown them.

4 The first group to guess the answer and correctly say the sentence wins a point.

5 Then the next person in each group has a chance to read one of your sentences and draw the information for their group.

6 Continue until all group members have had a chance to participate.

Having fun in nature: sentences

1 He/She is flying **over** a mountain.
2 He/She is jumping **in** a river.
3 He/She is riding **around** an island on a bike.
4 He/She is running **on** a beach.
5 He/She is swimming **under** the sea.
6 He/She is swimming **across** a lake.
7 He/She is walking **behind** a waterfall.
8 He/She is sitting **on** a mountain.

Grammar

6.4 I see . . . You see

From *The Standby Book: Activities for the language classroom* edited by Seth Lindstromberg

Outline	Students write sentences about a picture beginning 'I see' or 'You see'
Author's comment	Like many good, structured writing exercises this one should ideally end in speaking and listening – with each student hearing some of the sentences written by members of other pairs or groups. Note that the pictures referred to below can be photocopies or digital versions. Although this activity is basically for grammar practice, 'I see . . . You see' can also result in incidental vocabulary learning. At higher levels it works well either as a warm-up or as a useful fluency exercise for early finishers of some longer activity.
Editors' comment	This could also be done online, with students accessing the pictures and writing text under them on their digital devices using tools like Canva, or photo-captioning apps, or shared noticeboards like Padlet. If the activity is done in a conventional classroom, however, it's probably more effective to use paper, as suggested here. The pictures with the texts can then be displayed on the classroom wall.
Level	Elementary to Pre-intermediate (A2–B1)
Preparation	A varied assortment of interesting pictures that show landscapes and scenes with people, with space below to write

Procedure

1 Hand out your pictures, and allow people time to sort through them and choose one each that they like.

2 Meanwhile, write the following sentence starters on the board:

I am . . .
I can see . . .
I can hear . . .
I feel . . .
I . . .

3 Ask students to imagine they are in the pictures they have chosen and then to write five sentences, one starting: *I am . . .* , one starting: *I can see . . .* and so on.

4 In pairs, students swap papers. Each writes on their partner's paper three new sentences beginning *You . . . .*

5 Students swap their papers back, read and discuss.

Acknowledgement
This activity is attributed to John Morgan.

100 Great Activities: The Best of the Cambridge Handbooks for Language Teachers

6.5 Let's have a drink

From *Dialogue Activities: Exploring spoken interaction in the language class* by
Nick Bilbrough

Outline	A student makes a suggestion to the class and the idea is responded to positively with actions
Author's comment	I've always been interested in alternative ways of doing drilling and I particularly like this variant because of the way it combines physicality, gesture and emotion with what is essentially a very controlled activity.
Editors' comment	Research has shown that coordinating language with actions makes the language more easily internalized and recalled and – surprisingly – this is true not only for those performing the actions but those witnessing the actions being performed.
Level	Pre-intermediate to Upper Intermediate (B1–B2)
Preparation	None

Procedure

1   Invite the students to stand up, preferably where there is a little bit of space to move.

2   Give them a possible continuation for the sentence head *Let's . . .* , (e.g. *Let's have a drink*). The students then respond in unison with the reply, *Yes, let's have a drink*, before they all mime the action. Nominate a student to think of a different continuation, and the process continues until each student has had at least one turn at choosing a sentence.

Variation

At higher levels a greater range of language for making suggestions can be used (*Why don't we . . .* , *It'd be a good idea to . . .* , *I think we should . . .* , *How about . . .* , etc.).

Acknowledgement

I first learnt this exercise from Jon Trevor in a games workshop at the Friends' Institute, Highgate, Birmingham.

Grammar

6.6 Miming adverbs

From *Five-Minute Activities: A resource book of short activities* by Penny Ur and
Andrew Wright

Outline	Students perform simple actions in the manner of a given adverb
Authors' comment	This is a good way of practising *-ly* manner adverbs, and a fun activity for the end of a lesson. You can ask two students to go outside and then come back to give the commands and guess what the adverb was (it's easier for two students to think of and give commands than it is for one, and less stressful). This targets mainly classes at elementary level, but can be done as a fun 'filler' for more advanced classes (see the Variation).
Editors' comment	Lots of fun – Scott has played this with groups of friends. Not so easy – to comb your hair *archly*!
Level	Elementary to Intermediate (A2–B1+)
Preparation	None

Procedure

1 One student goes outside, and the others choose a manner adverb (for example, 'quickly' or 'angrily').

2 The student returns and orders one of the members of the class to do an action by saying, for example, *Stand up!* or *Write your name on the board!* or *Open the door!*

3 The person addressed has to carry out the command according to the manner adverb chosen: to stand up quickly, or write their name angrily, for example.

4 The student guesses what the adverb was, or if he or she can't guess, continues to give commands.

Miming adverbs

Elementary to Pre-intermediate adverbs: quickly, slowly, angrily, sadly, happily, quietly, loudly, lightly, heavily, strongly, funnily

Pre-intermediate to Intermediate adverbs: calmly, lazily, sleepily, fearfully, proudly, secretly, silently, painfully, lightly, seriously

---

Variation

The same activity can be used with advanced classes, practising the addition of the *-ly* (or *-ally* after *-ic*) suffix to adjectives. In this version, the 'acting' students are allowed also to speak, as long as they don't mention the target adverb or its corresponding adjective. Some adverbs that might be used:

dramatically, gracefully, decisively, apologetically, worriedly, thoughtfully, stiffly, jerkily, childishly, drunkenly, unwillingly.

100 Great Activities: The Best of the Cambridge Handbooks for Language Teachers

6.7 Oh!

From *Grammar Practice Activities: A practical guide for teachers* by Penny Ur

Outline	Students create sentences in the present perfect to express what has just happened to produce a given response
Author's comment	If I were asked what's my favourite grammar practice activity from this book, I'd probably choose this one. It's fun, it's a welcome departure from conventional sentence-completion exercises, and generates a lot of meaningful practice of the target structure. As a follow-up, you might also find it interesting to invite students to compare the exclamations in English with their equivalents in the students' own language.
Editors' comment	Who said grammar practice can't be fun? And, of course, you could adapt this activity to other grammar structures, such as *going to*, quite easily: 'I'm going to get married next week!'
Level	Pre-intermediate to Upper Intermediate (B1–B2)
Preparation	A list of exclamations, as the example below, displayed on the board, shown on individual digital devices, or distributed to students on paper

Procedure

1 Show or distribute copies of the series of exclamations and make sure everyone understands them.

2 Ask students to choose one and say what they think has just happened to make the speaker say it.

3 For example, 'Oh!' might mean that:

She has had a surprise.
Or
He has just remembered something.

4 Elicit a couple of examples to serve as models, and then tell students to write down what they think has just happened for as many of the exclamations as they can. They can choose whichever they like, in whatever order they like. Give them about ten minutes to do this.

5 Invite a student to read out one of their sentences without telling the rest of the class what the exclamation was that gave rise to it.

6 The rest of the class (and you!) try to guess which exclamation was intended.

154

Grammar

Exclamations

1 Oh!	11 Great!	21 (sigh)
2 Wow!	12 What a shame!	22 No, thank you!
3 Oh good!	13 I'm sorry!	23 Rubbish!
4 That's funny!	14 Oh no!	24 Thank goodness!
5 Congratulations!	15 Yes!!!	25 Touch wood!
6 Cool!	16 Yes?	26 Well?
7 Yes, please!	17 Hallo!	27 Unbelievable!
8 What?	18 Never mind!	28 Bad luck!
9 Stop it!	19 Thank you!	29 Cheers!
10 Ouch!	20 Welcome!	30 Goodbye!

From *100 Great Activities* © Cambridge University Press and Assessment 2024   PHOTOCOPIABLE

Note

In my experience, sooner or later the students start making funny combinations which produce a laugh. If a student has produced the sentence 'I've just got married', for example, based on the exclamation 'Congratulations!', there is usually a humorist in the class who will suggest that the appropriate response is 'What a shame!' or 'Never mind!'

Variation

To make this activity a little simpler, use only the first 20 exclamations.

100 Great Activities: The Best of the Cambridge Handbooks for Language Teachers

6.8 Question stories

From *Games for Language Learning 3rd edition* by Andrew Wright, David Betteridge and Michael Buckby

Outline	The teacher asks students questions which later serve as the basis for a story they will write
Authors' comment	This technique of storymaking can be used profitably at any level. It is better if you, as teacher, keep control of the collecting and retelling of the stories in order to keep the momentum of the drama going. However, students can be asked to retell the story, for example, the next day.
Editors' comment	It's quite difficult to remember all the answers to the questions, so you might write up very brief note-form answers to the questions you ask on the board. Then students can compose the story either orally (in the full class or in small groups), or in writing (individually or in small groups) using the notes on the board as prompts. Note that often the students will call out different answers to questions: so you might like to write up more than one answer, and allow students to choose which they want to use in their final stories.
Level	Elementary to Intermediate (A2–B1+)
Preparation	None

Procedure

1 Tell the learners that they are going to make a story and you are going to help by asking questions. Tell them that anything you ask about must be included in the story.

2 Ask questions such as the following:

Who is in your story? A man? A woman? A boy? A girl? An animal?
(Then ask a few details about the person/animal they choose.)
Where is he/she/it at the beginning of the story?
(Ask them to be precise even to a particular location, for example: *On the lowest branch of a big tree in a park in the middle of a city.*)
When does the story begin? (season, month, day, time)
What is the weather like?
What is he/she/it doing?

3 Follow by using a variety of questions in order to help the drama to unfold, for example:

What's he/she/it doing now?
Something happens. What is it?
Some people are watching him/her/it. Who are they? What do they want?

4 Students compose the story in the present or past tense.

Follow-up
The following day you can ask the class to reconstruct and retell the story.

156

Grammar

Variations

1 Question stories based on pictures
You will need pictures of people, places, etc. Display the pictures on the classroom wall, or project them on the screen. Tell the learners that the pictures are illustrations for their story, and that they must make a story to fit the pictures. Use the same question technique as above.

2 Question stories based on objects
You will need a collection of objects. Show the objects to the learners. Ask them to make a story inspired by the objects. Use the same question technique as above.

3 Question stories based on a single word or phrase
Write a single noun or verb on the board. Tell the learners that they must make up a story based on the word. Use the same question technique as above, for example:

Starting word: *man/woman*
What does this man/woman look like?
What is he/she doing?
Where is he/she?
What's his/her problem? etc.

4 Question stories based on phrase or sentences.
Write a whole phrase or sentence on the board. For example: *He's/She's crying*; or *It was very valuable*; or *The wind was blowing*; or *There was silence.*

157

100 Great Activities: The Best of the Cambridge Handbooks for Language Teachers

6.9 Sentence repetition

From *Testing Spoken Language: A handbook of oral testing techniques* by Nic Underhill

Outline	Students are challenged to repeat sentences that they hear
Author's comment	This is a quick and effective test, which although neither authentic nor communicative, can discriminate well at all levels of ability. The easiest way to score is just to mark each sentence right or wrong, and to count up the number right over 10 or 12 sentences; this requires no special training for assessors.
Editors' comment	It may seem surprising that an apparently 'mechanical' test is in fact valid, but research evidence indicates that its results correlate well with results of other types of assessment. The reason is that normally we cannot accurately repeat (or, indeed, write down from dictation) sentences we don't understand: so this test is likely to be a reliable indicator of level of comprehension.
Level	Beginner to Intermediate (A1–B1+)
Preparation	A set of phrases or sentences at an appropriate level

Procedure

1 The learner hears a series of sentences or utterances and repeats them as accurately as he or she can. The sentences may be read out by the interviewer or they may be recorded. These can be randomly chosen, or could exemplify specific language areas, such as structural or functional points covered in the syllabus or specific items of vocabulary.

2 Sentence length can vary from one word (e.g. 'Hello!') to 15 or 20 words; sentences above this length are rare in natural speech, and difficult even for advanced speakers to repeat correctly.

Variations

1 At higher levels, and with longer sentences, where language processing is clearly involved, there is a good argument for rewarding repetitions which have the same meaning but employ different words or structures. For example, if the stimulus sentence is:

> *He said he was hoping to come this weekend, but as it turned out he wasn't able to.*

and the learner replies:

> *He said he was hoping to come this weekend, but in fact he couldn't.*

that could be regarded as a fairly acceptable repetition. Rewarding meaningful paraphrase in this way would seem to make the test more valid, but involves a degree of judgement of acceptability on the part of the assessor that straight right-or-wrong repetition marking does not.

2 Gradually increase the amount to be memorized. The sequence of sentences for repetition begins with one- or two-word utterances and the length progressively increases, one word at a time, until the learner gives a repetition which is clearly incorrect. Another sentence of the same length is given, and if that too is repeated incorrectly, the repetition task ends there. The number of words in the last successfully completed sentence can be used as the score. Quite a lot of trial and error will be necessary in the test construction process to get a variety of sentences which are, in practice, in order of increasing difficulty. Differences of familiarity of vocabulary and complexity of structure can make short sentences difficult and long ones easy.

158

Grammar

6.10 Student-generated test

From *Learner Autonomy: A guide to developing learner responsibility* by Agota Scharle and Anita Szabo

Outline	Groups write a test for the class
Authors' comment	This activity encourages students to see a test for what it is: a means of measuring their knowledge or identifying problem areas, and something which is useful for them, too, and not only for the teacher. Preparing a test and discussing difficulties arising with peers may require more time than studying for a teacher-written test, but it may considerably increase students' understanding of the material.
Editors' comment	Some teachers claim that if students compose their own tests, then they'll know the answers so it isn't really a test. We think it is, because it still requires students to check their own knowledge, and is a valuable tool for formative assessment, as the authors explain above. It also lowers test anxiety, and gives students a feeling of 'ownership' of the assessment procedure.
Level	Elementary to Advanced (A2–C1)
Preparation	None

Procedure

1   You may start by asking students what items of grammar or vocabulary they found most useful or important over the given period, and decide together what should be included in the test.

2   Then assign each set of items to a pair or group of students and ask them to prepare a test. You may provide a set framework (e.g. multiple choice sentences for which they write choices, or a text for a cloze test), a few patterns to choose from, or give them total freedom concerning form.

3   Depending on the complexity of the material they have to work on, pairs or groups may finish their work during the lesson, or may do the task for homework.

4   Next, collect the completed test pieces and make any necessary corrections. You may combine the pieces into one comprehensive test which you give to the whole class or use only selected components from each contribution. Then correct and mark them yourself or together with the whole class.

5   If you don't want to use the test results to evaluate individual performance, you can ask groups to work on the test together.

Variation

You may make each group responsible for the administration of their bit of the test: in this case students get the test items on separate slips of paper or in a separate section of a digital assessment tool (and only the ones written by some other group), and when they have finished everything, they give their answers to the authors of the test item for correction. This may result in some confusion if there are more than three or four groups, so you may need to help by collecting and redistributing answers and then returning the corrected answers to each student.

159

100 Great Activities: The Best of the Cambridge Handbooks for Language Teachers

6.11 What can you do with it?

From *Games for Language Learning 3rd edition* by Andrew Wright, David Betteridge and Michael Buckby

Outline	Students suggest original uses for an everyday object
Authors' comment	This game works best if you encourage fun and invention.
Editors' comment	It's best for this activity to use actual objects rather than written descriptions or even pictures. After doing the activity described here, you might then divide the class into groups, give each the same kind of object (a pen, for example, or a tin can), and then challenge them to think of as many uses as they can. After five or ten minutes, the class comes together to pool ideas and perhaps see which group had the most, or the most original, ideas.
Level	Elementary to Advanced (A2–C1)
Preparation	Prepare a set of objects or write a list of objects on the board: for example, a paper bag, a hammer, a pram, an empty tin can, a mirror, a table.

Procedure

1 Reveal each object in turn to the learners.

2 Ask the learners to imagine different things which could be done with the objects, for example:

Teacher: *How can you use a paper bag?*
Learner 1: *You can put things in it.*
Teacher: *Yes, what else can you do with a paper bag?*
Learner 2: *You can light a fire with it.*
Teacher: *Yes. Anything else?*
Learner 3: *You can blow in it and then make a bang!*
Teacher: *Lovely! What else?*
Learner 4: *You could make it into a ball and throw it at someone to attract their attention!*

Variation

1 You might find it supports the learners if you write key phrases on the board:

You can ... You could ...

Or more extended sentence patterns:

You can/could make ... with it.

2 Put the students into small groups, give each an object and challenge them to think of, and write down, as many uses for it as they can. Later, pool and compare results: which group had the most suggestions, or the most original ones?

Cambridge Handbooks for Language Teachers: Complete Series List

Adrian du Plessis, Commissioning editor

Drama Techniques in Language Learning: A resource book of communication activities for language teachers by Alan Maley and Alan Duff — 9 November 1978

Games for Language Learning by Andrew Wright, David Betteridge and Michael Buckby — 20 September 1979

Michael Swan, Series editor 1981–1989

Discussions that Work: Task-centred fluency practice by Penny Ur — 30 January 1981

Drama Techniques in Language Learning: A resource book of communication activities for language teachers 2nd edition by Alan Maley and Alan Duff — 20 January 1983

Once upon a Time: Using stories in the language classroom by John Morgan and Mario Rinvolucri — 24 November 1983

Teaching Listening Comprehension by Penny Ur — 9 February 1984

Games for Language Learning 2nd edition by Andrew Wright, David Betteridge and Michael Buckby — 17 May 1984

Keep Talking: Communicative fluency activities for language teaching by Friederike Klippel — 14 February 1985

Working with Words: A guide to teaching and learning vocabulary by Ruth Gairns and Stuart Redman — 15 May 1986

Testing Spoken Language: A handbook of oral testing techniques by Nic Underhill — 28 May 1987

Learner English: A teacher's guide to interference and other problems by Michael Swan and Bernard Smith — 11 June 1987

Literature in the Language Classroom by Joanne Collie and Stephen Slater — 17 December 1987

Dictation: New methods, New possibilities by Paul Davis and Mario Rinvolucri — 15 December 1988

Grammar Practice Activities: A practical guide for teachers by Penny Ur — 15 December 1988

The Inward Ear: Poetry in the language classroom by Alan Maley and Alan Duff — 19 October 1989

Pictures for Language Learning by Andrew Wright — 16 November 1989

Five-Minute Activities: A resource book of short activities by Penny Ur and Andrew Wright — 6 February 1992

100 Great Activities: The Best of the Cambridge Handbooks for Language Teachers

Penny Ur, Series editor 1995–2005

The Standby Book: Activities for the language classroom edited by Seth Lindstromberg	4 September 1997
Lessons from Nothing: Activities for language teaching with limited time and resources by Bruce Marsland	9 July 1998
Beginning to Write: Writing activities for elementary and intermediate learners by Arthur Brookes and Peter Grundy	21 January 1999
Ways of Doing: Students explore their everyday and classroom processes by Paul Davis, Barbara Garside and Mario Rinvolucri	11 February 1999
Using Newspapers in the Classroom by Paul Sanderson	22 April 1999
Teaching English Spelling: A practical guide by Ruth Shemesh and Sheila Waller	27 January 2000
Teaching Adult Second Language Learners by Heather McKay and Abigail Tom	23 March 2000
Personalizing Language Learning by Griff Griffiths and Kathy Keohane	20 July 2000
Teach Business English by Sylvie Donna	27 July 2000
Learner Autonomy: A guide to developing learner responsibility by Agota Scharle and Anita Szabo	17 August 2000
Using Folktales by Eric K. Taylor	31 August 2000
The Internet and the Language Classroom by Gavin Dudeney	21 September 2000
Planning Lessons and Courses: Designing sequences of work for the language classroom by Tessa Woodward	8 February 2001
Learner English: A teacher's guide to interference and other problems 2nd edition by Michael Swan and Bernard Smith	26 April 2001
Using the Board in the Language Classroom by Jeannine Dobbs	3 May 2001
Teaching Large Multilevel Classes by Natalie Hess	12 July 2001
Writing Simple Poems: Pattern poetry for language acquisition by Vicki L. Holmes and Margaret R. Moulton	13 September 2001
Laughing Matters by Péter Medgyes	11 April 2002
Stories: Narrative activities for the language classroom by Ruth Wajnryb	3 April 2003
Using Authentic Video in the Language Classroom by Jane Sherman	17 April 2003
Language Activities for Teenagers edited by Seth Lindstromberg	18 March 2004
Pronunciation Practice Activities by Martin Hewings	29 April 2004
Extensive Reading Activities for Teaching Language by Julian Bamford and Richard R. Day	21 October 2004
Five-Minute Activities for Business English by Paul Emmerson and Nick Hamilton	3 March 2005

Scott Thornbury, Series editor 2005–

Drama Techniques: A resource book of communication activities for language teachers 3rd edition by Alan Maley and Alan Duff	24 March 2005
Games for Language Learning 3rd edition by Andrew Wright, David Betteridge and Michael Buckby	16 February 2006

Cambridge Handbooks for Language Teachers: Complete Series List

The Internet and the Language Classroom: A practical guide for teachers 2nd edition by Gavin Dudeney	8 March 2007
Dialogue Activities: Exploring spoken interaction in the language class by Nick Bilbrough	22 March 2007
Five-Minute Activities for Young Learners by Penny McKay and Jenni Guse	5 April 2007
Dictionary Activities by Cindy Leaney	10 May 2007
Working with Images: A resource book for the language classroom by Ben Goldstein	18 December 2008
Grammar Practice Activities: A practical guide for teachers 2nd edition by Penny Ur	2 April 2009
Intercultural Language Activities by John Corbett	14 January 2010
Learning One-to-One by Ingrid Wisniewska	19 August 2010
Communicative Activities for EAP by Jenni Guse	6 January 2011
Memory Activities for Language Learning by Nick Bilbrough	10 March 2011
Vocabulary Activities by Penny Ur	22 December 2011
Classroom Management Techniques by Jim Scrivener	23 February 2012
CLIL Activities: A resource for subject and language teachers by Liz Dale and Rosie Tanner	12 March 2012
Language Learning with Technology: Ideas for integrating technology in the classroom by Graham Stanley	4 April 2013
Translation and Own-language Activities by Philip Kerr	27 March 2014
Language Learning with Digital Video by Ben Goldstein and Paul Driver	6 November 2014
Discussions and More: Oral fluency practice in the classroom by Penny Ur	27 November 2014
Interaction Online: Creative activities for blended learning by Lindsay Clandfield and Jill Hadfield	2 February 2017
Activities for Very Young Learners by Herbert Puchta and Karen Elliott	9 March 2017
Teaching and Developing Reading Skills by Peter Watkins	14 December 2017
Lexical Grammar: Activities for teaching chunks and exploring patterns by Leo Selivan	31 May 2018
Off the Page: Activities to bring lessons alive and enhance learning by Craig Thaine	5 November 2020
Teaching in Challenging Circumstances by Chris Sowton	18 March 2021
Teaching and Developing Writing Skills by Craig Thaine	13 April 2023

Index

Main headings in **bold** refer to activity names.

30-second stimulus talks 6–7

A long and growing list 128–129
An A–Z of signs in English 80–81
academic English (for EAP classes)
    Course evaluation 17
    Delayed reverse translations 105–106
    Input enhancement 139–140
    PMI 42
    Predictive listening 74–75
    Summarising the summary 125
    Using symbols 88–89
Acrostic 94–95
action-based activities *see* movement-based
    activities
adjectives
    Adjectives on the internet 148
    Association webs 130–131
    Cinquain 99–100
    Desirable qualities 133–134
    How do they rank? 27
    How many things can you think
        of that … ? 138
adolescents *see* teenagers
adverbs
    Association webs 130–131
    Miming adverbs 153
    Once upon a time 116
    Pass it round 144–145
    Search a page 146
AI-generated text 125, 148
Alibi 8–9
All-purpose needs check 10–11
Altering and marking 64–65
animal guessing game 26
assessment
    Sentence repetition 158

    Student-generated test 159
    see also feedback
Association webs 130–131
autobiographical activities
    It happened to me 70
    Numbers in my life 38–39
    Simple selfies 123–124
    The teacher's autobiography 77
    Three things about me 56
autonomy *see* learner autonomy

Becoming a picture 12–13
beginners, activities for
    Altering and marking 64–65
    Association webs 130–131
    Bingo 96
    Change chairs 66
    Chants 14–15
    Circle comparisons 149
    Classroom language 84–85
    Describe and draw 18
    Do you remember? 135
    Drawing my natural world 150
    Flashing 24
    Foodies 108–109
    Ground-plans 67–68
    Guess them fast! 136–137
    Interrupting the story 69
    A long and growing list 128–129
    Looking up words you know 141
    Making mine long 114
    Name them 36–37
    Obeying instructions 72
    Oral retelling by students 73
    Say things about a picture 46–48
    Search a page 146
    Sentence repetition 158

Index

Simple selfies 123–124
Talk like a robot 76
True or false 78
Bingo 96
Bouncing dialogue 97–98
business English
All-purpose needs check 10–11
Interview interrogatives 28–29
Management tips 32

Cambridge Handbooks for Language Teachers 1–2
complete series list 161–163
Celebrity dinner party 82–83
Change chairs 66
Chants 14–15
ChatGPT *see* AI-generated text
Cinquain 99–100
Circle comparisons 149
Classroom language 84–85
Collective story writing 101
Comment on the comments 102
Congratulations 16
Connect two 132
Course evaluation 17
course planning 17
Creative copying 103–104

Delayed reverse translations 105–106
Describe and draw 18
Desirable qualities 133–134
Dialogue interpretation 19–20
dictionary use 115, 141
Dictogloss 107
digital learning
An A–Z of signs in English 80–81
Adjectives on the internet 148
All-purpose needs check 10–11
Celebrity dinner party 82–83
Comment on the comments 102
Flashing 24
Foodies 108–109
Jumbled statements 71

Recorded stories 45
Simple selfies 123–124
Spoken journals 53–54
Strip cloze 86–87
Direct Method 72
Discussion group tag 21
distance learning *see* digital learning
Do you remember? 135
Drawing my natural world 150
drawings *see* picture-based activities

easy activities *see* beginners, activities for
English for Academic Purposes (EAP) *see* academic English
evaluation *see* assessment; feedback

fairy tales activity 119–120
feedback
All-purpose needs check 10–11
Comment on the comments 102
Course evaluation 17
Spoken journals 53–54
see also assessment
Find someone who 22–23
Flashing 24
fluency *see* speaking activities
Foodies 108–109

games
Alibi 8–9
Bingo 96
Find someone who 22–23
Guess the animal in 20 questions 26
Guess them fast! 136–137
How many things can you think of that … ? 138
A long and growing list 128–129
Miming adverbs 153
Obeying instructions 72
Say things about a picture 46–48
Secret topic 49
True or false 78
What can you do with it? 160

100 Great Activities: The Best of the Cambridge Handbooks for Language Teachers

Getting students to ask the questions 25
grammar activities 3–4 *see* all the activities in
    the Grammar section from pages
    147–160, and in addition those from
    other sections listed below
    Alibi 8–9
    Chants 14–15
    Cinquain 99–100
    Guess the animal in 20 questions 26
    How do they rank? 27
    Interrupting the story 69
    Interview interrogatives 28–29
    Opinion poll 40–41
    Oral retelling by students 73
    Sad consequences 122
    Self-directed interviews 50
Ground-plans 67–68
Guess the animal in 20 questions 26
Guess them fast! 136–137

How do they rank? 27
How many things can you think
    of that … ? 138

I am … 110–111
I can't spell that! 112
I see … you see 151
ice-breaker activities
    Congratulations 16
    Find someone who 22–23
    Numbers in my life 38–39
    Self-directed interviews 50
    Simple selfies 123–124
    Speed dating 51–52
    Three things about me 56
    What do we have in common? 59–60
images *see* pictures
information gap principle 57–58
-ing form of the verb 99–100
Input enhancement 139–140
Interrupting the story 69
Interview interrogatives 28–29
It happened to me 70

jazz chants 14–15
journals 53–54
Jumbled statements 71

learner autonomy 3, 54, 112, 159
Let's have a drink 152
Letters 113
listening activities 3–4 *see* all the activities in
    the Listening section from pages 63–78,
    and in addition those from other sections
    listed below
    Dictogloss 107
    Running dictation 121
    Search a page 146
    Sentence repetition 158
    Tell me my story 55
Looking up words you know 141

Make them say it 30–31
Making mine long 114
Management tips 32
Map-reading: the treasure hunt 33–34
materials-light *see* no materials needed
memory-based activities
    Alibi 8–9
    Dictogloss 107
    Do you remember? 135
    A long and growing list 128–129
    Oral retelling by students 73
    Sentence repetition 158
Miming adverbs 153
Mini-stories 115
movement-based activities
    An A–Z of signs in English 80–81
    Change chairs 66
    Congratulations 16
    Discussion group tag 21
    Find someone who 22–23
    Let's have a drink 152
    Miming adverbs 153
    Obeying instructions 72
    Running dictation 121
    Speed dating 51–52
    Talk like a robot 76

Index

multilingualism
    An A–Z of signs in English 80–81
    Delayed reverse translations 105–106
Multipart story drama 35

Name them 36–37
no materials needed
    30-second stimulus talks 6–7
    An A–Z of signs in English 80–81
    Alibi 8–9
    Change chairs 66
    Discussion group tag 21
    Getting students to ask the questions 25
    Guess the animal in 20 questions 26
    Interrupting the story 69
    It happened to me 70
    Let's have a drink 152
    Miming adverbs 153
    Obeying instructions 72
    Secret topic 49
    Talk like a robot 76
Numbers in my life 38–39

Obeying instructions
Obeying instructions 72
Odd one out 142–143
Oh! 154–155
Once upon a time 116
one-to-one activities
    Tell me my story 55
    What do we have in common? 59–60
online learning *see* digital learning
Opinion poll 40–41
Oral retelling by students 73

Paper talk 117–118
Pass it round 144–145
picture-based activities
    Altering and marking 64–65
    Becoming a picture 12–13
    Describe and draw 18
    Drawing my natural world 150
    Flashing 24
    Foodies 108–109

    Ground-plans 67–68
    I am … 110–111
    I see … you see 151
    Say things about a picture 46–48
    Simple selfies 123–124
    Thoughts 126
    What are the differences? 57–58
PMI 42
poetry
    Acrostic 94–95
    Cinquain 99–100
    I am … 110–111
    Vanishing stories 90–91
Point of view 119–120
Predictive listening 74–75
present participles 99–100
pronunciation activities
    Guess the animal in 20 questions 26
    Pronouncing places, products and planets
        43–44
    True or false 78
Pronouncing places, products and planets
    43–44
proper nouns 43–44

Question stories 156–157

reading activities 3–4 *see* all the activities in the
    Reading section from pages 79–91, and in
    addition those from other sections listed
    below
    Comment on the comments 102
    Creative copying 103–104
    Delayed reverse translations 105–106
    Dialogue interpretation 19–20
    Find someone who 22–23
    Foodies 108–109
    I can't spell that 112
    PMI 42
    Running dictation 121
    Search a page 146
    Summarising the summary 125
recall *see* memory-based activities

167

100 Great Activities: The Best of the Cambridge Handbooks for Language Teachers

Recorded stories 45
remote learning *see* digital learning
reverse translation 105–106
rhythm activity 14–15
robot activity 76
role play
    Alibi
    Becoming a picture 12–13
    I am … 110–111
    Interview interrogatives 28–29
    Multipart story drama 35
    Point of view 119–120
    Talk like a robot 76
    Why do you have a monkey in your bag? 61
Running dictation 3, 121

Sad consequences 122
Say things about a picture 46–48
Search a page 146
Secret topic 49
Self-directed interviews 50
selfies activity 123–124
sentence expansion activity 114
sentence patterns activities 72, 128–129, 160
Sentence repetition 158
short fillers
    30-second stimulus talks 6–7
    Creative copying 103–104
    Flashing 24
    How many things can you think
        of that … ? 138
    I see … you see 151
    Interrupting the story 69
    Let's have a drink 152
    Miming adverbs 153
    Obeying instructions 72
    Why do you have a monkey in your bag? 61
Simple selfies 123–124
social media 123–124
    see also digital learning
speaking activities 3–4 *see* all the activities in
    the Speaking section from pages 5–61,
    and in addition those from other sections
    listed below

Circle comparisons 149
Dictogloss 107
Guess them fast! 136–137
I see … you see 151
Interrupting the story 69
It happened to me 70
Let's have a drink 152
Oh! 154–155
Oral retelling by students 73
Running dictation 121
Talk like a robot 76
What can you do with it? 160
Speed dating 51–52
spelling
    Acrostic 94–95
    Bingo 96
    Do you remember? 135
    I can't spell that! 112
    Pronouncing places, products and planets
        43–44
Spoken journals 53–54
spot the difference activity 57–58
stimulus talks activity 6–7
stories
    Collective story writing 101
    Interrupting the story 69
    It happened to me 70
    Mini-stories 115
    Multipart story drama 35
    Once upon a time 116
    Oral retelling by students 73
    Pass it round 144–145
    Point of view 119–120
    Predictive listening 74–75
    Question stories 156–157
    Recorded stories 45
    Tell me my story 55
    Vanishing stories 90–91
Strip cloze 86–87
Student-generated test 159
Summarising the summary 125
symbols activity 88–89

168

Index

Talk like a robot 76
The teacher's autobiography 77
Tell me my story 55
testing *see* assessment
Thoughts 126
Three things about me 56
Total Physical Response (TPR) 72, 76
treasure hunt activity 33–34
True or false 78

Using symbols 88–89

Vanishing stories 90–91
video drama 71, 102
virtual learning environments (VLEs)
    see digital learning
vocabulary activities 3–4 *see* all the activities in
    the Vocabulary section from pages
    127–146, and in addition those from
    other sections listed below
    Acrostic 94–95
    Bingo 96
    Chants 14–15
    Cinquain 99–100
    Classroom language 84–85
    Creative copying 103–104
    Guess the animal in 20 questions 26
    How do they rank? 27
    I can't spell that 112
    Make them say it 30–31
    Predictive listening 74–75
    Pronouncing places, products
      and planets 43–44
    Sad consequences 122
    Say things about a picture 46–48
    Secret topic 49
    Tell me my story 55

warmers *see* ice-breaker activities
What are the differences? 57–58

What can you do with it? 160
What do we have in common? 59–60
Why do you have a monkey in your bag? 61
writing activities 3–4 *see* all the activities in
    the Writing section from pages 93–126,
    and in addition those from other sections
    listed below
    All-purpose needs check 10–11
    Congratulations 16
    Course evaluation 17
    Interview interrogatives 28–29
    Management tips 32
    Opinion poll 40–41
    Pass it round 144–145
    Self-directed interviews 50
    Student-generated test 159
    Three things about me 56
    What can you do with it? 160

young learners
    Association webs 130–131
    Bingo 96
    Change chairs 66
    Chants 14–15
    Describe and draw 18
    Drawing my natural world 150
    Flashing 24
    Guess the animal in 20 questions 26
    Interrupting the story 69
    A long and growing list 128–129
    Miming adverbs 153
    Numbers in my life 38–39
    Obeying instructions 72
    Say things about a picture 46–48
    Talk like a robot 76